Letters

to

Uncle Fred

Assorted short stories
With commentary ranging
from insightful to silly
(An occasional diatribe)
Intended to entertain and amuse

Ronald Villanova

Llumina Press

ISBN: 1-59526-375-6

Printed in the United States of America by Llumina Press

Library of Congress Control Number: 2006924518

To Roberta

Photos

Preface

My uncle Fred was very dear to me. During the latter part of his life, half a continent separated us. Visits were infrequent, but we stayed in touch by phone and letter. Written communications were more effective for me because, whether on the phone or in person, he tended to dominate the conversation with his views, stories and commentary on virtually anything from opera to philosophy to - his favorite topic - World War II (he was a Pacific theater combat vet). An intelligent, well-educated, articulate and kindly man, his humor often strayed to the acerbic, with portraits of persons and events embellished and exaggerated for emphasis.

In my letters to him, I adopted his sense of humor and the absurd. This pleased him and afforded him the opportunity to reply with scathing critiques of my rationale, style, grammar and syntax. It was all in good fun. My purpose was to entertain him and to make him laugh; an attempt to repay him in some small way for the attention, love and kindness he had shown me all my life.

He understood, and the reader should also, that the letters were (and are) not intended as documentaries. The events and persons portrayed are based on fact, but the original letters have been redacted. Moreover, even in the originals, certain liberties (quite a few actually) were taken with the facts, and some of the characters are composites of two or more persons. Some of the footnotes were in the original letters, and some added later for the benefit of my children and grandchildren, to translate foreign language phrases, explain abbreviations, military jargon or the like. Uncle Fred needed no such aid. Those that are original and those that have been added should be clear from the context.

Table of Contents

Letters

to

Uncle Fred

The Beginning

Dear Uncle Fred,

I believe enough time has passed since I last wrote you, to waste your time with another missal. There have, in the interim, been many public and private events that might be noteworthy. However, I continue to remain subject to my spouse's admonition to relate to you some of our more interesting (at least to us) experiences. With such a charge, and such a wealth of mildly to extremely odd incidents to draw on, I have some difficulty in knowing where to begin or end. The result is, as you've probably noticed and as my spouse and children have expressly indicated, that I tend to ramble almost incoherently in a more or less stream of consciousness manner, with little regard to structure and proper sequence.

I acknowledge the accuracy of the criticism, and although I will make every effort to do better in that regard, at bottom I really don't care. This is my letter and I'll write it any way I see fit. If they don't like it, they can write their own letter. I shall proceed. I've decided to tell you a bit of the process whereby I became a lawyer. Yes, it's a long story; but no, I won't spare you the detail.

I'm sure that at some point during your long life you've noticed that seemingly minor events can have long term consequences.

Many years ago, when I was a beardless youth, I worked on a farm owned by Roberta's grandparents, Clara and Fred. Clara was a strong-minded, hard working, god fearing woman, well within the stereotypical Yankee tradition. She was also a very nice (e.g., kind, compassionate) woman. Her husband, Fred, was a horse of a different stripe. Fred was some 20 years Clara's senior and where she was warm, he was cold; where she

was kind, he was nasty; where she was nice, he was sarcastic; where she was gentle, he was brutish. You get the picture.

Fred was always ancient. From the time I first became aware of him he was old, very old. But I was young, and having no history with the man, I did not avoid him as most of his children and neighbors did. I really couldn't avoid him anyway. It was his place and I was working there. Fred was in the habit of strolling around the place, visiting the barn and the milk room while I was working. He didn't speak very often; an occasional grunt served as a greeting, or at least an acknowledgment that I existed and had appeared in his line of sight.

On these forays he always carried a fly swatter, it being his primary hobby apparently, to kill as many flies as possible. There was no dearth of the disgusting, annoying insects in the barn, due to the constant and volu-minous defecation of the 60 or so Jersey cows in said barn. Fred's secret weapon in this deadly pursuit was his ability to fart (proudly and loudly) at will, thus providing an olfactory lure for the flies to meet their doom in his vicinity.

Sometimes, I would sit on the milk room stoop and Fred would take a similar position next to me. On one such occasion, the normal silence of these vigils was interrupted by the appearance in the yard of a brand new '58, green, Chevy Impala. A clean-shaven young man with a brush cut got out of the car and approached us. He wore no jacket, but his pants were obviously the lower segment of a suit; his shirt was white, and he wore a conservative tie, neatly pulled fully to his throat.

"Good afternoon, sir." He smiled at the old man, who remained silent as, without lifting his head, he simply raised his eyes to the man.

"I was wondering if you could tell me where I might find the Salter family."

"Never heard of 'em," said the old man.

"Oh, I was told they lived near this farm," the man persisted.

"Maybe you were told that, but I never heard of 'em," the old man insisted.

"Well, … okay, … thanks." He left.

As he left, I asked the old man why he had done that. After all, the Sal-ters lived up the dirt road no more than a quarter mile away. "Dago (that's what he called me), never tell a stranger nothin'," he said. Now, you may be asking yourself, and justifiably so, what this has to do with becoming a law-yer. Be patient, I think I can connect it up.

The old man, as I've indicated, was taciturn. When he spoke it was usually a brief, highly distilled, conclusion from his long life of careful observation of the human experience and the characteristics composing the essential nature of certain individuals; as when, interrupting a prolonged discussion between Clara and one of her friends about his cousin Jim, he said "He's a dumb shit," and remained silent for the rest of the day. I couldn't think of anything that summed Jim up any better. On this basis I tended to grant credence to such gems as "never tell a stranger nothing," "he's a dumb shit," and "if your feet are cold put your hat on," and looked for the facts behind his conclusions. It was this respect for his credibility that permitted me to take his statement of other conclusions in the spirit with which they were intended.

"Dago, ... ya' know, you're just one step above a negra."

This statement was made without animosity, without prejudice and without any hint of being anything other than a simple statement of his conclusion based on observed fact. He paused, then rocking himself to one side, released a poisonous vapor into the air, and continued:

"Yeah, ... you're so low, you got no place to go but up. How you doin' in school?"

Now, I suppose one would not be unreasonable to take offense to these reflections on one's station in life; but the facts were that I was earning $1 per hour, milking cows - pitching hay and shoveling mountains of dung - hardly a foundation from which one might dispute the conclusion. He was right. The reference to school was not really a question. He knew, because observation had been his life ever since he retired from his position of the town's postmaster, that I attended school infrequently. In fact, that second semester of my junior year I would set the record (which I have reason to believe still stands) for the greatest number of days (45) of absence ever accrued by a high school student who ultimately graduated with his class.

I said, "My grades are good; I just don't want to be there." He was getting to his feet, releasing more vapors in the process, and without looking back as he left, asked, "You want to be here?"

There was no need for reply; to ask the question was to answer it. I didn't want to be there, and I didn't want to be here. Some sort of change had to be formulated and implemented. I had some unanticipated help in doing that.

Mr. Nickerson was my guidance counselor, a task he found most frustrating. He had summoned me to his office so often by way of the morning announcements that my homeroom classmates would finish the litany of those so summoned by a chorus of "and Villanova, Ronald A." It was a tired tale. He asserted that I had to attend classes, otherwise I would not be allowed to continue, and what a shame that would be because I was such a good student, but I lacked discipline, and what would my family think, and why was I throwing my future away, and failing to grasp the opportunity, and don't understand why, how could I be so, don't you know what it, etc. etc., etc. To all of this I stood mute; and when asked to speak would only say:

"This place makes me puke."

How could I tell this good man, who had expended his entire life force in a vain and futile attempt to educate the most dull member of each of his classes, that he had it all wrong; that he, and every other teacher, should relegate the invincibly stupid to vocational schools and focus on teaching those who were capable of learning? I couldn't. It would have destroyed his world-view; I didn't want that on my conscience. Besides, I never tell a stranger anything.

Mr. Nickerson couldn't handle it. As my absenteeism escalated he became irrational. There were a number of incidents that semester that were of sufficient gravity that the principal, Mr. McGarry himself, addressed the student body during morning announcements. It seems that acts of vandalism were being perpetrated by a certain despicable "element" within the school, and when he discovered the members of that "element" he would deal most harshly with them. The acts continued despite these threats and McGarry continued to decry them, vowing vengeance on what was now commonly known as "The Element." Mr. Nickerson took it into his head that The Element was composed of deviant thugs who must be, had to be because they could not be caught, led by a superior intelligence who controlled them like some teenage Svengali and guided their clandestine and nefarious activities; in short, an intelligent malcontent: Villanova, Ronald A.

Through public announcement, Mr. Nickerson demanded that I see him. I didn't; I wasn't there. He demanded again; to no avail; same reason. He instructed my homeroom teacher to send me directly to his office "the moment he shows his face." I waited until the start of first class to show him my face. He was unhappy, he informed me.

"Villanova, you have gone too far, and this time you won't get away with it. I have determined through a series of necessary inferences that The Element is a bunch of rats and that you, Villanova, are the king rat. Oh, you may have Lorraine [Mrs. Labonte, my homeroom teacher] and Sandra [Mrs. Pederson, my history teacher] fooled; but you don't fool me.

No sir, you don't fool me. I know what you're up to. You're using those rats to make me look bad, to make this school look bad. You 're trying to create havoc, chaos, disrespect for authority, my authority - all authority! You're tearing down the very institution that has done its best to nurture you and every other goddam ungrateful bastard that bounces in here, and I have you right where I want you!!

What do you have to say for yourself, mister!!??"

"This place makes me puke," I said.

"That comment proves it, mister. I want you out of this office. I want you out of this building. I want you **out, out, out!!!**"

Mr. Nickerson was not in a good mood. He was, in fact, a bit over the edge, or as we said in those days, he had one tire in the dirt. But he had been a Jarhead[1] during the war, so I said, "I respectfully request that I be allowed to speak to your commanding officer, Sir."

---

[1] A Marine

Hesitation. His eyes shift rapidly side to side. He smiles, sort of.

"Allowed? ... Allowed? ... Mister, ... I'll take you right to him."

And he did. Mr. McGarry was chunky of body, round of face, and devoid of scalp hair. He was in his mid-forties, a seasoned administrator who, through his obvious intelligence, good nature and gentle, but no nonsense manner, had risen rapidly in the system. I trusted him; my trust was not misplaced. Mr. Nickerson was, for all practical purposes, without the ability to communicate in a clear manner, though his attempts to explain his agitated state, particularly as to how I had instigated that state and nearly every incident of misfeasance, malfeasance and tortfeasance known in the history of the school, managed to make some mark on McGarry. McGarry assured Nickerson that he understood and that he would take it from here, suggesting that Nickerson spend a little time in the teacher's lounge before resuming his normal duties.

"So what was that about, Villanova?"

"Sir, Mr. Nickerson is hysterical."

"Hysterical is a strong word. He's 'upset.' Why do you suppose he's upset?"

"He thinks I'm the king rat, sir."

"And just what is 'the king rat', Villanova?"

"The leader of The Element, Sir."

"Are you?"

"No."

"How do I know that?"

"If you check my attendance, sir, you'll find that I'm not here enough to organize a poker game, let alone some intricate conspiracy to discredit this institution and everyone in it."

"I know all about your attendance, or rather the lack thereof, Villanova. What, then, do you suppose is the basis for Mr. Nickerson's allegations?"

"Battle fatigue, Sir?"

"Now, now, I'll hear none of that. Just what did you do, or say, that set him off?"

"I told him this place makes me puke."

"And does it?"

"Yes, Sir."

"Would you care to expand on that condition? I think I need an explanation."

"It's really simple, sir. I don't want to be here because I don't need to be here to learn what I need to learn to pass the tests. All I do is read the book; show up when tests are scheduled; take the test; pass it; then read for the next test. Why should I go to class if I don't have to?"

"An interesting perspective, but it so happens that we have rules, and one of them relates to attendance, and you've violated that rule more often than any other person in the history of this school. On the other hand, you're consistently on the honor roll, which is the only reason I've allowed you to remain on the student list. Now, do you want to discuss the conditions for my continued forbearance in staying the rule in your case?"

"May I have my lawyer present?"

"No, you may not have your lawyer present! Where do you think you are? Do you think I'm some kind of monument to the freekin' Constitution? This isn't a judicial proceeding; this is my school! I'm the judge. I'm the jury. I'm the prosecutor, and right now I'm the only freekin' defender you've got!"

He seemed to be "upset," so I decided to humor him. I stood mute.

"What do you have to say?" he demanded.

"This place makes me puke."

I saw a faint movement at the corners of his mouth. He exhaled slowly, and just as slowly reached behind him to a file cabinet and pulled out a file that said in big black letters: **Villanova, Ronald A.**

"Quite a file I've got on you. Quite a file. Let's see, what have we got here? Says here that you've scored in the top 10% of every aptitude test we've forced you to take. Says here that you're on the honor roll; that you don't work up to your potential and that you demonstrate an open disdain for authority; that your attendance is abysmal (which I knew already); and that you've steadfastly refused to apply to take the college entrance exams, despite the fact that you are clearly college material [this wasn't true. I had already taken the SATs and scored well enough to virtually assure my acceptance at several colleges. I maintained the refusal posture only to aggravate Mr. Nickerson] There's a note in here from Mrs. Furdy demanding that you be expelled for wearing your work clothes in class, and another from Mr. Abruzzi demanding that you be expelled for throwing magnesium into a sink in his chemistry lab. [It really does burn in water] Any explanation?"

"Teenage high-jinx, Sir?"

"Not good enough, Villanova. Let's cut to the chase here, son. I've got to do something about you. Guys like you are a menace to the efficient administration of this institution. You don't want to follow the rules; you don't want to play the game; you don't want to do what you're told. Suppose nobody followed the rules? What then?"

"Then, I guess it would be foolish for me to follow them. Wouldn't it?"

"Don't get smart with me, son. On the basis of your attendance alone I could expel you. Which brings me to the matter of your absences from detention. It says here that you have never stayed for detention; never, ever, not once. And this despite the fact that you, at this very moment, owe me, let's see ... why, you owe me 1,250 hours of detention!! How the hell do you explain that?"

"Mathematics, sir."

"Mathematics? What the hell are you talking about, son?"

"It's mathematics, sir. Each time I decline to attend detention, the amount of detention time is doubled. The progression is geometric, rather than arithmetic, which produces the ridiculous number you just mentioned. At this rate I would, if I agreed to do so silly a thing, which I don't, spend the next five years of my life in detention."

"I understand math! What do you mean you 'decline to attend'?"

"Just that. I decline."

"Detention isn't an invitation, Villanova. It's a demand; it's a rule; you've got to 'attend'!! Why do you refuse to follow the rules!?"

"This place makes me puke, sir."

"No, no, no. Nu-oh. You're not going to do that to me, you manipulating little shit. This isn't Bartleby the Scrivener. You can't just say 'I prefer not to' and do whatever you want. We're going to settle this right now. Here's the deal. I'll waive the detention, remove the expulsion request from your file and overlook the absences. The condition is that you will accept writing assignments from me. I'm going to scrutinize them closely. Any failure in quality, or any failure to complete the assignments on time, and I'll kick your scrawny butt out of here so hard you'll land in Connecticut." [a distance of some 25 miles]

Writing assignments? Oh, no, anything but that. Please don't throw me in the briar patch.

"One more time, Villanova, are you the king rat; any rat at all?"

"No. And no. Categorically."

That was the absolute truth. I had no more knowledge of The Element than he or Nickerson had. For all I knew The Element was composed of members of the cheerleading squad. I knew only a relative handful of the other inmates in that place. For most of those I felt nothing but indifference; they could all go to hell in a hand basket, as far I was concerned. For a few, I had an intense dislike; those I simply declared non-existent. As for the rest I had a mild interest, but only for the purpose of distraction from the unmitigated monotony and enervating boredom.

High school would not, however, be my most anti-intellectual experience; that would come in law school (but that's a different story).

In any event, there it was: conflict, crisis, confrontation, compromise, nonviolent resolution; each side believed it had won. It was elegant in its symmetry. It was a pattern that would emerge many times in my future.

The first assignment was a thousand words on "The Inside of a Tennis Ball." There is much to be said of the contents of a tennis ball; e.g., the composition of its gases, their molecular structure; their discoverers; their uses; etc., etc. It should have been entitled "A Piece of Cake." The next assignment was 2,000 words on "The Dorr Rebellion." Not much of a rebellion, but an event of local historical note and charm. The confrontation between the rebels and the state militia had taken place on Cemetery Hill, in Chepachet. Not much of a confrontation either. The rebs dispersed and their leader fled to Connecticut when the federalies showed up. I used this little paper as my submission to the Grange for their annual college aid competition. The prize went toward my college tuition. The paper should have been sub-titled: "How I Made $100 in an Hour and a Half."

Ronald Villanova

The assignments became successively more complex, arcane and of greater length as McGarry sought to punish me. Of course, the entire teaching staff knew of the arrangement and as the subject matter became more obscure I began to make more intensive use of the library. The library, what a wondrous place.

Stacks full of books, most of which had remained untouched by human hands for decades, just waiting for me to wipe the dusty accumulations of disuse away and read them; to plagiarize their contents; and bring their information into the light. The smell of the library was sweet, and musty. I inhaled its scent; I participated in its quiet. I used it as a non-rebuttable excuse for skipping classes: "I'm working on something for Mr. McGarry." Life is good.

I think McGarry hoped that the final assignment would be the blockbuster, the chunk of ice in my peaceful sea that would sink me. It was 10,000 words to answer the question: "Was the Revocation of the Massachusetts Charter in 1684 Justified?" I didn't know that there was a Charter, let alone that it was revoked, and I didn't have the foggiest idea whether it was justifiably voided. I determined that it would be a start to see the Charter. It wasn't available in the library. The librarian (who was under the impression that I was "such a diligent student") located several books that made reference to the revocation, but no description of the terms of the Charter itself appeared. I called the Boston Public Library (on the school phone). I told the lady who answered that I was doing some research for my Master's dissertation and would love her forever if she could help me find the Charter (she fell for it; librarians are fairly gullible). She told me that because it was an official State document, copies were available and she would send me one that very day. I gave her my home address.

The Charter was in English, but an archaic form, and filled with so many "whereas," "hereinafters," "thereuntos," mysterious Latin phrases, and convoluted syntactical ambiguities that it occurred to me it must have been drafted by a master of obfuscation: a lawyer. As I studied the document, the code began to show itself; one word will not do, there must be four or five that mean almost the same thing, but not quite; tautologies are mandatory; the word "said" must be used at least once in any operative sentence, and does not extinguish the mandatory tautology rule; the same word must not always carry the same sense, and its connotation may be freely exchanged and hopefully obscured by its normal denotation; Latin phrases are to be liberally employed, particularly where the concept is easily conveyed by an English equivalent which suffers from a lack of majesty. Now this was up my alley, so to speak.

Lawyers for each side conducted the debate between the English brass and their colonial vassals. Clearly, the facts disclosed that the Charter had been, as the brass asserted, more honored in the breach than the observance. Nevertheless, the colonial lawyers mounded up heaps of words structured to deflect the charges, to make black appear - if not white, then at least - gray, to put a humble, subservient, slant on even the most outrageously inappropriate and illegal (under the Charter) behavior. How did they do that? They were constructing arguments from the ether. They twisted and tormented the language of the Charter. They ignored certain facts and created others as needed to suit their objective. They were terrific lawyers. It was almost believable.

Almost.

Was the revocation justified? Well ... sure. The group of misfits that then inhabited Massachusetts had been, or descended from, the scum of English society. A more vile congregation of wild-eyed, radical, hypocrites would be virtually impossible to assemble. If the brass in England had any sense of what was really going on in the colony, they would have been justified in binding everyone of them, hanging millstones around their necks and casting them into the utmost depths of the sea. At least that was my opinion.

But it was impossible not to be fascinated by the inventiveness and downright, blatant prevarication by the lawyers. No wonder McGarry was so threatened when I asked to have my lawyer present. If lawyers had that kind of license - that power - to create, to bamboozle, to play fast and loose with the truth, do it all in the name of protecting their clients' interests, and get paid for it too, then - hot-damn - I wanted to play in that game. The rules could be twisted, were expected to be twisted, to produce whatever shaped result was desired. Lawyers told other people what to do.

I decided that I wanted to be a lawyer. I kept that decision a secret, disclosing it only when, in college, they demanded to know my concentration and I was constrained to tell them: pre-legal.

The paper found favor with McGarry (as it eventually would with my History 2.02 professor at college). I was partially released from bondage. Under a new agreement with McGarry, I attended some classes 3 to 4 days a week; others not at all except to take exams. Mr. Nickerson no longer summoned me; he no longer spoke to me; he no longer looked at me. Too bad, I felt bad for the guy. It wasn't until after I was graduated that I spoke with him again. I telephoned him at home during the summer.

"Hello."

"Hello, Mr. Nickerson, this is Villanova, Ronald A."

"Who? The king rat?"

"Yes, Sir."

"What do you want?"

"I want to tell you that I've been accepted and plan to attend college in the fall."

"Well, isn't that just ducky. The king rat is going to college. Why should I care? Why did you feel I had to have this priceless information?"

"I thought I owed you something."

"Villanova, you make me puke." [Clunk – bzzz]

Hey, I tried.

I did tell the old man what was going on. Not that he asked. I just felt I needed to say something during those awkward silences on the milk room stoop, and I ended up telling him about Mr. Nickerson's bout with having one tire in the dirt, the deal that McGarry and I had struck, and my decision to become a lawyer. Why not, he wasn't going to say anything to anybody.

"A liar, huh."

"Yeah, a lawyer."

"I said liar, boy."

"Different."

"Same thing, Dago, same thing ... means you'll have to go to school a long time to learn how to do it. I mean, there's a certain way you gotta operate to make people happy while you pick their pocket. Sure you want to do that?"

"The school part no, not really; but if it's a way out of here I'm going to give it my best shot."

"You'll screw up. ... But anyway, it's good to have a dream, Dago ... good to have a dream."

The old man became ill while I was in my second year of law school. He had been "failing," as they used to say. The family packed him off to the hospital, where he stayed a few days, and was sent packing back home. The doctors said there was nothing they could do for him there that couldn't be done at home. He was dying; not of anything in particular, just dying. About a week later (I'm told, I wasn't there and can't attest to the accuracy of this) he was sitting in his chair, fly-swatter in hand, apparently dozing, when he rocked up on one hip, expelled one last measure of noxious gas and quietly expired, letting slip the fly-swatter to the floor. Seems right that he would die like he lived.

Roberta and I attended the wake. Her mother was there. She had cut out the newspaper notice of the old man's death, and had been sticking the piece of paper in peoples' faces as if the fact that it was in print made it official and elevated his demise to an historical event. I took it from her for something to do, and to prevent her from further embarrassing herself. There, mixed in among the things I knew, was the statement that the old man was a graduate of Nichols College. This was news to me. It had never entered my mind that the old man might have a college education. I checked with Robert (Roberta's father, the old man's son) who confirmed the newspaper account.

"I'll be damned! You old bastard!"

I made my way as nonchalantly as possible toward the casket. It was easy. Nobody was paying me, or the body, any mind. I stood at the head of the casket. I looked down at the old man. He seemed to be smirking at me. I smirked back, slipped a fly swatter out of my jacket and into the box. Maybe there are flies where he's going. Old bastard.

Harmon Manufacturing

Dear Uncle Fred,

I hope this finds you as well as can be expected under the circumstances. I also hope that sufficient time has elapsed that you have recovered from my last letter and are now in a frame of mind that will allow you to read this one without fear and loathing.

A recent series of events has given me reason to again observe that incidents in my life have a habit of doubling back on themselves. To explain why I say that will require some patience on your part, and the expenditure of some ink (or whatever it is in my printer) on mine. I'm going to go back more than three decades, so settle back in your Lay-Z-boy and shut off that damn TV. I will eventually connect this all up.

In 1960 I sought employment with Harmon Mfg. Co., Inc. in Grayville, Connecticut. The plant was one of three HMC locations. I went to this one because they were hiring for second shift. I was at school (college) during regular working hours, so second shift was what I wanted. I went over to Grayville. I've mentioned before the economically depressed conditions that exist in the area that straddles the R.I. - Conn. border (sometimes called "Little Appalachia").

The once booming mill towns were, in 1960 and now, little more than villages comprised of old, formerly company-owned houses, clustered around a decaying hulk that once was a textile factory. Grayville was just such a village, with the significant difference that its hulking factory - although obviously decayed - was still functioning within its original purpose. I went into the office and asked the woman at the desk for an employment application. "Don't have any," she said, "You want a job?" "Yeah" said I, "second shift." "You'll hafta talk ta Gerry. He's ovuh theyuh."

So I went over there to talk to Gerry. I told him I wanted a job on second shift; any job he might have. He asked: "Are you 18? Got your own car?" I was 18 and had a '48 Ford so I answered "Yeah." He asked: "You afraid of work?" I answered no.

"I got a job on the baling crew. Want it?"

"Yeah."

"Know what a baling crew does?"

"No."

"You care?"

"No."

"Good. You got a job kid. When can you start?"

"Anytime."

"How 'bout tomorrow?"

"Fine."

"OK. Be here at 3. Talk to Del. By the way what's your name?"

"Ron Villanova."

"Vilnew? "

"No, Villanova."

"What is that? Spanish?"

"No, my ancestors came from Italy."

"Hey. Whatever. It's Vilnew to me."

Fine. I showed up the next day before three and found "Del." Del was the second shift supervisor. Del was in his mid-fifties, about my height, had several days' growth of beard, dressed in a dark green shirt with dark green pants, and wore a dark green, duck-billed, cap. He spoke English with a French-by-way-of-Canada accent. I found out later that his name was Adelard Beauregard and "Gerry" was Gerard Gaudreau. They called me Rol Vilnew. Whatever.

Del had me sign some pieces of paper, then took me over and introduced me to my baling crew partners: Rudy and Herb. This was going to be an experience. Rudy was about 6 feet 2 or 3 inches tall, weighed about 250 and had a handshake that I felt in my shoulder. Herb was just a bit taller than I (about 5' 9") but was built like a refrigerator. I figured he also went 250 pounds. Don't let anyone tell you that the Neanderthals expired without leaving their genes in the Cro Magnon stock. Herb's wrists were the size of my ankles, his shoulders were twice the width of mine, and he had muscles on his muscles. I decided it would be best to get along with this formidable duo. The first thing Rudy said (addressed to Herb) was "Oh, chrise, another Cannuk." "No" I said, "Italian."

"Oh, christ," said Herb (to Rudy) "worse, a guinea." This wasn't going to be easy. "Never mine dat shit," said Del. "You guys jus' teach 'im de ropes. I want 25 bales outta ya, so no flippin' the duck." [Flippin' the duck?? Must be a trade term.]. Del went off.

"Don' worry, guinea, we'll teach ya the ropes," Herb informed me. "Bitch is, with you here the quota's 25 now." "Yeah," says Rudy, "they give us a skinny guinea, an' think we can do twice as much. Sonabitches." Actually, 25 was more than twice as much. A two-man crew was expected to produce 12 bales in 8 hours, but a 3-man crew was expected to produce 25. Just how Jerry and Del had come to this conclusion wasn't explained; but, hey, when you're making $1.27 an hour (2 cents/hr "premium" for second shift) and happy for it, you don't ask.

Now let me bore the bejuzzuz out of you by explaining "the ropes." We were baling "fiber stock." The fiber stock was mostly nylon, but sometimes rayon. It was "crimped" and cut into short lengths upstairs on the third floor, then blown through ducts down to the first floor into one of six cavernous "bins" from which the crew hauled it in arms full to the bale-press. The bale-press was a hole in the floor some 10 feet deep, about five feet long and two feet wide. The hole was lined with steel and at its bottom was a steel plate mounted on a huge hydraulic cylinder. Above the floor were four hinged concrete and steel doors that continued the shaft about three feet above floor level when closed. Over these doors was a massive cast iron and steel top plate mounted on rails. The top was rolled over the shaft opening by means of a manually operated, chain driven system of pulleys and gears.

Of course, there was no such thing as an Occupational Safety and Health Act at that time. This machine and virtually every other machine in the place were designed for brute efficiency; safety devices were rudimentary or non-existent; and every job in the plant was hazardous. If there had been an OSHA, the plant would have been shut down.

So, the job was to place a piece of burlap on the bottom plate when that plate was in the full-up position; turn a valve that released the water in the cylinder to drop that plate; close three doors and fill the hole with fiber stock; then close the remaining door and fill the above-floor with fiber stock; put burlap over the hole, roll the top plate over and turn on the pump. Depending on the amount and type of fiber stock, the pump would take two to four minutes to squash it into the intended bale. We'd then open the doors, being careful to stand to the side to avoid the, sometimes, explosive force of the pressure on the doors. Then we'd fix the burlap to the sides of the bale with ice-picks and place wires around the bale (both the bottom and top plate were slotted to accommodate the wires) remove the picks, then release enough pressure to roll back the top plate and extract the bale by rocking it onto a hand truck. We finished the bale by "capping" the ends with more burlap secured by wires or strapping. Each finished bale was tagged to indicate type and weight.

A bale could weigh between 400 and 700 pounds depending on type, some types being denser and more easily compacted than others. The lighter bales were dangerous because of the greater amount of potential energy stored in their "springy" fiber stock. All that energy could be released by the failure of a single wire. There was no danger from the fiber stock itself; the danger was in the wires. If one wire went, the others usually followed in a cascade of whipping steel that sounded like incoming automatic weapon fire and could flay your skin into multiple painful welts. Rudy had a bad back. He handled the light bales.

This work did not require an awful lot of thought. It was perfect.

Working conditions were, however, something less than ideal. The air was constantly filled with dust from the blown fiber stock and from the dirt and decaying wood of the ceiling above us that served as the floor for the spinning "frames" on the second floor. The vibration from those machines sent us a steady shower of such particles along with dripping oil. The final touch to air quality was the proximity of the dye "house," from which wafted the smell of ammonia, chlorine and other noxious chemicals. Dyed stock had to be dried, so there were two 30 feet long, oil-fired dryers that expelled most of their excess heat into the surrounding area. There was no air conditioning. We worked stripped to the waist, even in winter; covered in sweat-caked dust and clinging bits of fiber stock; breathing particulates and toxic gases; killing off more brain cells than I care to think about.

Learning the ropes took a few bales. It took longer to learn about Rudy and Herb; but not too long. Both were in their mid-thirties. Herb was not married, but lived with what we would now call a "significant other." He was a mild mannered guy, easy going, with a good sense of humor. He was also intelligent, well read, and a bit of a raconteur.

Rudy was married to a woman whose height almost equaled his own and whose weight exceeded his by maybe 50 pounds. She was BIG, with a pie shaped face and light blonde/brown hair that hung to the middle of her back. I always imagined her carrying a spear and wearing a horned helmet. She and Rudy had tried to have children. These attempts were tragic, producing still-born babies weighing between 12 and 14 pounds. Rudy was not intelligent, well spoken, or humorous. He was a decent, caring, sensitive guy whose difficult life and doomed desire for a child had left him in an almost uniform state of melancholy. He and Herb were good friends. Herb told me that Rudy couldn't read. Herb had tried to teach him, but thought that Rudy was so embarrassed by the effort that he wouldn't learn. In a rare act of charity I also tried to teach Rudy, at least enough to write out the bale tags, but it was apparent that he was dyslexic, a condition which I could not handle because I had no education, training or experience to do so.

I know, everybody has a sad story, but Rudy was a good guy and it was sad and frustrating that there was just nothing Herb and I could do for him. Of course, the owners of Harmon Manufacturing Inc. could not have cared less. They had a perfect employee; he wasn't going anywhere. Moreover, they had many other employees like Rudy and it would have been contrary to their interests to educate or otherwise assist any of them in a way that might cause them to think of themselves as something other than drones.

We weren't the only drones on the first floor. In addition to the two guys on the dye-house crew (who considered themselves somehow superior because they mixed chemicals - and better them than me) there were three other guys. One manned another bale-press; one ran a "super picker" and one ran a "chopper." The other bale-press was used only for dyed stock that had been processed by the "picker" located in the basement below us. It's output was considerably slower than the crimpers that fed us, so only one guy was normally required.

The chopper, you guessed it, was used to chop pieces of raw nylon that would otherwise be considered waste. It was this part of the operations at the mill that led old-timers to refer to it as a "shoddy" mill; a designation I thought pejorative until I learned that "shoddy" originally referred to the recycling of used woolen cloth or fiber into new. The first step in recovery of that material was to chop it into pieces that the super-picker could handle.

A super-picker is a machine composed of two steel drums; the first about 6 inches in diameter and four feet long; the second about three feet in diameter and of the same length. Both cylinders were covered with multiple rows of densely packed steel teeth. The first cylinder picked up the chopped nylon from a feed table and slowly brought it into contact with the teeth of the second cylinder. The second cylinder turned at an extremely high rate; probably about 3,000 rpm, producing a high pitched sustained shriek. The disparity between the number of revolutions of the first and second cylinder caused the material to be pulled and shredded by the whirring teeth of the latter into an almost cotton candy consistency.

This consistency was just what was needed by the "carding" machines (also on the second floor, near the spinning frames). The six carding machines were all manufactured well before the first world war. They were run by electric motors, but it was obvious that they were originally run by belts connected to a central shaft that ran the length of the second floor ceiling; and itself had been connected by a belt to a water wheel, which once existed outside the building. These machines were a marvelous maze of pulleys, gears, belts, cogs, dogs, cams and levers, with a score of toothed cylinders; all intended to form the cotton candy stock into something resembling a large spool of gauze.

The machines were inherently dangerous. The stock frequently jammed in their legion of mechanical contrivances. The operators were loath to stop the machine, so they often tried to extract the offending matter without doing so. This sometimes resulted in the loss of a finger or fingers to the machine's jagged maws; and there was hardly an operator (all men) who had all his digits intact. Thus, nicknames like "three-finger" Louie (pronounced, *treefinguh*), "lefty" Baptiste and "stubby" O'Donnell were factually descriptive rather than mere monickers.

The product of the carding machines was transferred to the spinning machines. As the name implies, these spun the gauze-like material into a thread. These machines, and the "twisters" which turned spun stock into a final product used largely in rug-making; were much more forgiving, and were operated exclusively by women (including, for a good number of years, the Me's spouse, Loretta).

Now, you're wondering why it is that I have described the process in such detail. There are several reasons. First, I wanted to make good on my promise to bore the bejessuz out of you. Second, I wanted to give you a picture of the barbaric conditions and primitive machinery. And third, I wanted to put the description down on paper so that if, through some quirk in the space-time continuum, this piece of paper survives for a hundred years, someone will know a little something of the machinery, the process and the conditions; by that time such knowledge will otherwise surely be lost.

As boring as all that may be - are you awake? - my fellow employees were truly a cast of characters. You may recall that my brother Dave (the Me) also worked in the mill. This was fortunate for me because he was a steady, reasonably sane ally throughout the almost three year experience at HMC. The Me did some of everything. He was more inclined to a multi-faceted responsibility than I. I didn't want to be bothered by an uncertain schedule. I wanted to work on the baling crew exclusively, for the simple reason that I could read my textbooks while the press was coming up (at 25 bales per eight hour shift, study time was at least an hour and a half). Besides, his acceptance of a more general responsibility toward the operations of the plant brought him into more frequent contact and conflict with its management. I preferred to keep my head down and pursue the crew's conflicts through stealth and deflection (call it subversion if you want) rather than confrontation. Let me give you an example.

Working with the same guys day after day in the circumstances I've outlined, tends to foster an "us" versus "them" perspective. It also produces what the current psychobabble crowd refers to as "bonding." That jerk jargon aside, I think you would agree with the statement of the simple fact that a small group of men in a difficult situation will do what they've got to do, not for anything abstract like god, country, mom or any other concept, ideal or principle, but for each other.

We knew we were being treated like shit; we resented it; but were virtually powerless to prevent it. I said "virtually."

Occasionally, the company would receive a large order that required prompt completion. On such occasions, Gerry would demand that we increase our output by 5 to 10 bales per shift. In these situations, management had the hammer, so to speak, because we were all employees at will and sufferance (as we say in the law) and we could be fired for any reason or no reason. We, of course, objected to such demands unless some additional compensation commensurate with the additional effort was forthcoming. These objections were met with stern admonitions to do it or get out. To his credit, the Me suggested that some monetary incentive would be appropriate, but management declined. Pleas to authority seldom succeed. When the third such situation arose during my tenure, we determined that a protest of some sort was in order. But what?

The basement of the mill was a dark and dank place in which a healthy colony of rats had existed for generations. The population of said rats was held in check by a combination of limited available nutrients and the presence of a small, but effective clan of feral cats. We knew of the subterranean predators and prey because it was our task to fix the hydraulic pump, piston and control devices whenever they malfunctioned (not often) and these were located in the basement.

In the event of a malfunction, we threw fingers to determine who would investigate and repair knowing that the loser risked an encounter with the rats or the cats. In fact, we were more wary of the cats. The rats would usually slink away at our arrival. The cats were a different story. They were large, dirty, mangy, ill tempered, territorial and, some said, rabid.

At the commencement of our shift we were instructed that the West Point order had to be filled "Now! Tirty-two bales is your quota. Don' give me no shit. No flippin' the duck. Jus' shut up an' do it." On our first bale, the pump stopped. We threw fingers. I lost. I practically begged Rudy to come with me, just to keep the cats away. He said "My heart pump [sic] piss for you, guinea." I understood that as a "no." I took several spool cores (aluminum cylinders about a foot long and an inch in diameter) to fend off the cats and headed into the basement. The setting was that of a gothic horror-movie. The way was lighted by 60-watt bulbs dangling from the wires that supplied them, spaced at 30-foot intervals. All the smells from above merged with the stench of excrement from the cats and rats below. The stones of the walls shined wet in the feeble light of the 60 watters.

I easily perceived that there was no problem with the massive piston itself. There was no gushing water in the pit that would indicate a breach in one of its gaskets. I looked up to the control arm attached to the electrical switch that deactivated the pump when the piston reached full top. There was a rat draped over it and near the rat was the ugliest, biggest, filthiest, bloodiest cat I'd ever seen. I instinctively hummed a spool at him - and missed. He sprang to my left, spitting and howling, as I threw another spool (another miss) while screaming profanity at the top of my lungs.

Kitty was dissuaded by the projectiles and screams to hunker down about 20 feet away and menace me with hissing, growling sounds. He was annoyed that I had interrupted his lunch. Rudy yelled down the shaft "Here, kitty-kitty. Come get a meatball for suppuh. ... You OK, guinea?" I replied "flip-off you polack pinhead," and heard Herb say, "He's OK."[2]

I had one spool left. Keeping kitty-kitty in my sideways sight I used it to flip the rat carcass off the control arm. I decided to bring Rudy a present. Using the spool core, I moved the rat onto a piece of burlap (pieces of burlap

---

[2] Actually Rudy was of Russian descent, and was offended by the notion that he was Polish. Therefore, we called him "Polack."

littered the place) and got out of there as fast as I could walking backwards, waving the spool with one hand, carrying the burlaped corpse in the other, and uttering guttural sounds with kitty-kitty yowling and advancing after me in a bizarre, atonal, interspecies disco dance.

Rudy did not appreciate his present: "Gawd, I hate that! Get that thing away from me! Jezzus chrise!" Herb was thoroughly amused by Rudy's reaction, but suggested that we dispose of the rat and get busy. The interruption had cost us time; we were already behind schedule. There was a discussion of what to do with the body and the unfairness of the increased quota. The discussion blended the two points into a consensus that the body should be placed in a bale. We partially filled the shaft, then performed the service of slipping the body out of the burlap and into the shaft as Rudy and Herb stood at attention on each side and saluted.

We made our quota. It did, of course, occur to us that there would be some consequence of some sort from our indelicate act of rebellion. Rudy fretted that we'd be fired; Herb anticipated a chewing-out, but nothing more. I believed the consequences to be wholly unpredictable.

A Digression

At the risk of aggravating your normal state of mind (irascible), I want to explain why I believed the consequences to be unpredictable. My major was pre-legal. That meant, in practice (I was then a sophomore and had not yet been allowed to take any pre-legal course) that my minor was philosophy. We were then surveying some of the big names in western philosophy, one of which was Hegel.

I don't know how much you remember about German philosophers, but my recollection is that they are, for the most part, a dreary and depressing lot. This is due, in no small part I'm sure, to the northern European latitude and climate that leads to a kind of madness caused by light deprivation.

According to Schopenhauer:

" ... the height of audacity in serving up pure nonsense, in stringing together senseless and extravagant words, such as had been known only in madhouses, was finally reached in Hegel, and became the instrument of the most bare-faced general mystification that has ever taken place, with a result which will appear fabulous to posterity and will remain as a monument to German stupidity."

Hegel is supposed to have said that "only one man understands me, and even he does not." I don't doubt it. My meager recollection of Hegel is that you would be hard pressed to find a more misspent piece of work in your lifetime. But don't take my word for it.

According to Durant, most of Hegel's writings are actually his lecture notes or, "worse," notes taken by his students. Only Logic and Phenomenology are his works and "these are masterpieces of obscurity, darkened by abstractness and condensation of style, by a weirdly original terminology, and by an over careful modification of every statement with a Gothic wealth of limiting clauses." Also, Durant says that "Hegel described his work as an 'attempt to teach philosophy to speak in German'. He succeeded."

I think those remarks refer to the "Hegelian dialectic" (what Fr. Cain[3] referred to as "Hegelian horseshit" and, more gently, "demented Darwinism"). That phrase is used to describe what seems to be the thrust of Hegel's philosophy; that is, that change is the basic principle of existence, nothing is permanent, contradiction is always present and resolution comes only through the "strife of opposition." Of course, like any other gross abstraction from the facts of existence, there is some truth in those propositions. But I think the facts of existence (experience) also show that you can take any such proposition too far.

The "strife of opposites" idea just didn't ring true. First, because it presupposes perpetual conflict, ignoring the observable fact that there is more cooperation in the world than conflict. Second, that "opposites" are the norm rather than the exception, as if for each idea or act there is a contradictory (as opposed to "different" or "contrary") idea or act. Third, that the cosmos and everything in it is deterministic; that is, a linear system, like a mathematical equation that will (because it must) produce a certain result. It is the particular falsity of this third aspect that caused me to agree with Fr. Cain's assessment of the "dialectic" and led me to conclude that the consequences of putting a rat in a bale were unpredictable. To explain why I say that calls for
…

A Further Digression

I have never had a taste for math. Oh, sure, I took the usual courses like geometry, algebra, trig and calculus, but I couldn't develop any keen interest. Certainly, such knowledge can be useful; e.g., from figuring out the checkbook to determining the present value of money. My lack of interest stems from my impression that the utility of math is limited to a stagnant model of reality. My forays into the use of math invariably produce a result that reflects the status quo or a projection of that status quo based on my assumptions of what the reality will be. This is unsatisfactory because I'm creating a future reality based on assumptions that are at best my largely uneducated guesses.

---

[3] My all time favorite college professor.

The result is preordained by those guesses, and the result is just another guess. My point is that math is fine in a linear system, but isn't useful in predicting future events in a dynamic system; that is, in reality.

So I agree with Hegel (not that he would, or you should, care) that change is constant, but I disagree wholeheartedly with the notion that change is driven by the strife of opposites and that strife is resolved by survival of one and annihilation of the "opposite." In a static system, maybe, in a dynamic system, no. The reason I say that is simple. In a system composed of human beings, the entities that constitute the system are individuals capable of making decisions and taking actions (rational or irrational, prudent or foolish) that affect some or all of the other individuals, and the system itself. Those decisions and actions can be so diverse, so complex, so variable and so capricious that no amount of advance mathematical calculation, no matter how sophisticated, could possibly predict an outcome to even the most seemingly trivial individual act (like putting a rat in a bale).

I suppose it is this non-linear, non-predictability which drew me to the practice of law, where the rules about the law remain fairly steady, but the outcome of a particular controversy can never be predicted with complete confidence and the result is unknown until the claims are actually faced within the particulars of the real world and allowed to work themselves out.

Hegelian philosophy has (with the exception of a few perverse pockets of insanity in some universities and boardrooms) been discredited and de-emphasized in most quarters.

End of Digression

When I arrived for work three days later, I noticed that the first shift guys were hanging around instead of preparing to run out of the place. When I asked what was going on, I was told that they had been instructed to stay because the owner's son wanted to talk to the baling crews together. Uh-oh. The owner's son was in his early thirties, clean cut, baby-faced, college educated and soft spoken. He was a good guy who didn't share his father's disdain for the serfs who operated his machinery. He was obviously perturbed about something. He said:

"Guys, something unpleasant has happened. I got a call from West Point. They said that one of our bales was ruined because it had a squashed rat in it. I think the guy I talked to was upset because a woman found the rat, rather than the fact that some stock was useless. Anyway, the thing is, I couldn't come up with an explanation for the rat. I know they're around here, but I don't know how one could've ended up in a bale. Maybe it croaked in the bin and one of you guys just picked it up and didn't notice. Maybe it was just one of those things, maybe not. Gerry can't explain it either, but he thinks maybe it wasn't an accident.

I'm not ready to accept that either. So we'll let this incident pass without further inquiry. But I don't want this to happen again. I want you all to be careful and make sure it doesn't happen again. Ya got me?"

We nodded or murmured our assent. The first shift guys left; we went to our station. Nobody said anything, but Herb kept a smirk on his face until Del came over. Del said:

"You guys ain't foolin' nobody, ay? We know where dat rat come from.[4] Where's all your brains at, one-time you? [I never understood the use of "one-time you" as the close to a question, as in the previous sentence or in, for example, "where's all your cigarettes at, one-time you?" I understood "side by each" for "next to," I even understood the use of the reflexive - e.g., "I don't care, me" - but "one-time you" remains a mystery.]

You guys been lucky you ain't fired. [talking to Herb and Rudy]: College-boy 'ere don't need dis job, but you two oughta tink about what happen' to you, ay?"

Rudy, his arms folded across his chest, took a step toward Del and said:

"Nobody betta mess with the guinea. Somebody mess with the guinea, maybe **he** ends up in a bale."

Del was dumbstruck by what appeared to be a wholly misdirected and hostile response to his concern for the non-college-boys' livelihood. Herb immediately recognized the potential for escalation and said, "What he means is that the guinea's got nothin' to do with anythin'. He works here just like us, and we're sick of bustin' our ass puttin' out extra bales and not gettin' paid for it."

Well, that framed the issue nicely. Del said, "you guys ah lucky you got a job," and walked away. "Sonsabitches," said Rudy, "stinkin' bastards." What struck me was that Rudy "needed" this job more than Herb or I, yet he was the most aggressive.

That night we didn't make our quota. I also didn't anticipate the reaction of the other bale-crews. The next day the first shift crew didn't make their quota. Nothing dramatic, just a few bales shy. Over the next few days there were a number of equipment failures that diminished production. Equipment problems cropped up in crimper, picker and carding machines. No one said a single word about a slow-down. There was no overt expression of any concerted action to reduce production; no scheme; no plot; nothing was said. The dynamic had changed.

After several weeks of silent protest, another rush order arrived. Gerry told us we had to make 30 bales and added, "Please do it. I'll make it up to ya." Please? I'll make it up to you? What was this about?

Fine. We decided to put out 30 bales, just to see what would happen. On Friday, in addition to our normal hours, we were paid three hours of overtime

---

[4] Indeed, it would be easy to find out; each crew had its own tags and our tag was on the bale.

(at time and a half - about $5.50). "Hey, guinea," Rudy said softly, "the eagle shit extra today." For the duration of my employment, the eagle shit extra whenever we were asked to exceed the normal quota.

I suppose that in the big scheme of things this doesn't qualify as a significant event. I also suppose a Hegelian would claim the incident as proof of his construct. He'd be wrong. What it proves, if anything, is that a trivial occurrence can ripple into a set of circumstances and produce an inordinate result; a result unanticipated by anyone's power of prediction at the time of the occurrence. I said I would connect this up. To do that, I'll vault forward about 34 years to late 1994. (There are other stories about working in the mill - I'll save them for later).

Last fall, Roberta's cousin Anne asked that we join her for supper. This was no ordinary invitation. Anne is self-employed as a cook, housekeeper, house sitter, and occasional general factotum for several well-to-do families in town. In her town there is a pocket of fine homes and hoighty-toighty prep and finishing schools for the offspring of the wealthy. Anne is not in that group. The invitation to supper was out of the ordinary because she was house sitting for one of her wealthy clients who was then vacationing (from his retirement) at his Aruba condo. We would thus dine with Anne at one of the mansions.

In this same time period, Roberta and I were heading toward my mother's house for a Sunday meal. I had called my mother and asked whether she could tolerate my presence for a few hours and, oh yeah, what's for lunch. She replied that she was making some pasta and calamari (what a surprise) and that she would accept my presence if I would leave my evil twin at home. I offered no assurance that the evil one could be so restrained. Anyway, we were on route 12, when I mentioned to Roberta that the area we were about to enter has always been one of my favorites. I explained that the little town had all the characteristics of classic New England: the white steepled protestant church, the cemetery, the village green (or "commons"), the federal style houses (some of which have been restored), all set on a bluff overlooking the valley.

Roberta seemed surprised by my comments, and indicated that she was attracted to the area as well, and for similar reasons. In particular, she said she had always wanted to go inside one of the houses facing the green. I had almost forgotten this house until she mentioned it. It does indeed face the green from behind a high fieldstone wall and numerous plantings. It is very large and distinctive. Its style is not colonial, not federal, and not Georgian; in fact I don't know the appropriate designation. I'd say it's Greek revival because of its external appearance (e.g., a colonnaded, formal front porch - a portico; two great rooms with curved exterior walls flanking a long and wide foyer) and because it was constructed during the 19th century.

As Roberta was lamenting that she had never been inside the house we came upon it and noticed a For Sale sign. Mere coincidence? She didn't think so. She wrote down the agent's telephone number. The next day Roberta called the telephone number, indicated the house we were interested in and arranged to meet with an agent on the afternoon of the day we were to dine with Anne. She was quizzed briefly by the person on the other end of the line about who we might be, what our station in life might be and why we were interested in this particular house. Roberta's cover story was that we were retired and looking into the possibility of opening a bed and breakfast. This satisfied the person and we were on.

We arrived at the real estate office on time. As we approached the office driveway, another car was in front of us indicating (by signal) an intention to pull into the same drive. The behavior of this vehicle aroused my attention because it couldn't seem to decide which portion of the highway it wanted to travel. I was suspicious that the signal might not disclose the true intent of its operator as it veered left and right, slowed, hesitated, sped up and slowed again. It did stop at a point, which matched the presumed signal intent but did not proceed into the driveway. Instead, it sat in the roadway; the only detectable motion being the quick, uneven wobbling of its operator's head. Suddenly it lurched forcibly to the left and entered the drive, the operator's head bobbing wildly as if this action were unanticipated. "Dumb bitch," I said. "It could be a man," said Roberta. "No it couldn't," I replied.

I followed the car into the parking area, keeping my distance as it came to an abrupt, nose-diving halt in front of the real estate office. From the car emerged a fifty-ish female, tall, with carefully tended and color enhanced hair, stylishly dressed and presenting, overall, a picture of the modern business woman. On closer scrutiny the picture showed a blouse partially pulled out of the skirt's waistband and an inside out and exposed skirt pocket. These modest defects were revealed as she struggled to free the pocketbook strap that had become entangled in the car's door handle when she exited (backward) from the car. She walked briskly toward the office. I parked a safe distance away. As we followed her in Roberta said, "I bet that's her." I said, "I bet she's a loony."

There was another woman in the office - an assistant of some kind. We introduced ourselves to the assistant while the "loon" excitedly moved papers around, chattering to no one in particular. The assistant managed to get the loon's attention, who now directed the chatter at us; a rapid-fire, high pitched stream of "how nice to meet you - I'm 'D.D.' - I've been so busy - weather is good - where are those papers - did anyone call - I've got another house for you - etc." She thrust a piece of paper at Roberta and went to her desk saying that we could look at the paper while she did something of extreme significance, and then she'd take us to the house.

Roberta looked puzzled. Through her teeth she whispered to me (pointing to the paper), "This isn't the house." I said, "Better make sure it's the right place before we go anywhere with her."

"Excuse me, DD. This isn't the house I want to see."

"Oh. ... Oh. ... Really? It isn't?"

"No, it isn't."

"Oh. ... Gosh. Oh. Which one are you looking at?"

"The wrong one."

"Which one?"

"This one in my hand is not the one I talked to you about."

"Oh. Oh, my. My gosh. Which one did we talk about?"

"The one on the Heights, across from the green."

"And that isn't it?"

"No, it isn't."

"Oh my. Gosh. I thought it was."

"It isn't."

At this point the assistant mercifully entered the discussion and told DD that we wanted to see the "Johnson house."

"Oh, really? Oh, my. The Johnson house? Well, I don't know. Oh my - well - sure you can see it. But it's a mess, it really is. A mess. Dear - dear. Oh yes."

The assistant wholeheartedly agreed:

"There are some people living there - not the owner - the woman is nasty and a slob. It's a mess."

DD continued:

"She tries to keep me from showing the place, and she let's her children run amok. She never cleans. I don't understand it. I don't think they pay any rent, and the owner pays the utilities, and they can't even keep it clean. Don't be shocked when you see it. It's a mess."

"So," I said, "what are you trying to tell me - that the place is a mess?"

"Oh, ... well ...yes. Dear -dear. Yes. It's a mess. Goodness, yes."

With that bit of information firmly entrenched, DD insisted that we ride with her because she had another place that was better suited for our purposes: a house that was being run as a B&B, which we'd visit after the sojourn to the Johnson house. Against our better judgment, we agreed, just to get on with it.

The Ford Escort station wagon bore the marks of numerous encounters with other objects. No serious damage, but a plethora of scratches, dents and dings had variously deformed, scoured and abraded virtually every piece of sheet metal on the vehicle. Even the roof had a curious set of engraved striations which I interpreted as tracks left by the contents of a grocery bag absentmindedly abandoned and cascaded by inertia when the vehicle was put into motion. Roberta sprinted into the back seat, forcing me to sit up front. I cinched up my seat belt.

The distance from the office to the house is about four miles. Four miles, that is, if you take the shortest route. DD chose a different route, first heading north (at speeds between 35 and 70 mph), then heading east on a back road (at speeds between 50 and 60 mph punctuated by random stabs at the brakes) until she found the Heights road. She then turned south (without stopping at the intersection - stop sign notwithstanding) maintaining a speed of 15 to 25 mph, while pointing out various houses; identifying who owned them; allowing the car to wander between the right hand shoulder and the shoulder of the on-coming lane; seemingly oblivious to the irritated motorists behind us who, to a man, extended and waved their fists at us - middle finger erect - as they passed to the right or left depending on which opportunity presented itself.

When we arrived some of the squatters were in the back yard. Clothed in a dirty T-shirt, ripped jeans and sandals, one straggle-haired, pot-bellied, tattooed member of the clan sulked away. A similarly festooned member approached, said hello to DD and called to the sulking figure, "Hey, Sherry, DD wants to show the house." To which Sherry replied, "Yeah, like I care." We didn't see her again. ·

DD chattered about the view and the outbuildings (in a sad state of disrepair) as she struggled to get in a side door. Failing that, we went around to the front door, for which she had a key. Still chattering, she struggled with the front door, calling to Eric - the male part of the tattooed duo - to help her. Eric opened the door from inside, apologizing that he had forgotten to unbolt it. In brief, the place was enormous (about 20 rooms) and at one time must have been the acme of residential splendor. All the floors were maple; all the moldings were oak; there were large fireplaces with marble stiles and mantels in the foyer and each of the great rooms that flanked it. This area of the house was used by the squatters' rug-rats as a play area. Their toys were scattered about, and marks from their big wheels showed on the floors and walls. Eric said that they had had about 100 people there for a Halloween party - which explained the sick smell of stale beer.

DD took us on a tour of the rest of the house, turning on every light she could find, and spewing a non-stop narrative in scrambled syntax, pausing only to express whispered criticism of the tattooed lady and her dismay about the deplorable lack of housekeeping. In our inspection of the multiple up-stairs bedrooms we surprised a number of other squatters encamped in some of them; mattresses were placed directly on the floor and the rudiments of an apparently nomadic lifestyle were strewn about said rooms. The place was being used as a flophouse.

We quickened our pace, completed the inspection and headed to the car. I appropriated the back seat. DD apologized several times before we cleared the driveway, promising to "do something about this" as she scraped the right side of the car against 50 feet of hedge.

Now she would take us to Killingly for a look at a completely reno-vated B&B; a house of historic significance, originally built in 1794. The dysfunctional driving continued. More motorists were annoyed into acts of frustrated negligence and rude gestures. DD took no note, even stopping dead - straddling the centerline on route 12 - to point something out to Roberta, who DD had finally discerned was familiar with the area and was related to the Sirrines.

"So, your grandmother was Melba?"

"Yes, that's what I said."

"Then you must know Herb."

"Herb's my uncle."

"Oh, my. Goodness me. Sure, I know the Sirrines, Herb is Anne's father. Right? Oh goodness, then you're Anne's cousin."

"Very good; yes we're cousins."

"So, who's your dad?"

"John."

"Really? Oh my. Gosh. Oh, for heaven's sake. I knew John. Sure, he did some work for us. What a nice guy! My little Tommy used to wait for him to come. He always shared his lunch."

"My father ate your son's lunch?"

"Oh ... oh, no. Goodness me. No. John shared his lunch with Tommy! Oh, my, isn't that something? John was your dad. Ya know, he would do some work and sometimes play with Tommy and then when my husband came home, sometimes he'd stay for supper and they'd have a few drinks, and sometimes they'd stay up 'til real late and tell stories and laugh, and oh my goodness."

"My father would keep Tommy up drinking 'til late?" [now Roberta's just putting her on]

"Oh my, no. I mean my husband."

"Great guy, my father."

"Oh my yes. And he died so young, so young. That's too bad. How did it happen?"

"He drank himself to death."

"Oh ... oh ... oh my. Dear- dear - dear."

We were now approaching the house we "had to see" so DD shifted the conversation to its owners, a Mr. and Mrs. Wilton. Mr. W is a retired UConn professor and Mrs. W an active professor at Brown University. They had run the place as a B&B for several years, but with their schedules (which included stays at the south coast of France) they didn't have the time, energy or inclination to continue the B&B operation. The house had been on the market for over a year without result, and they were willing to "talk price." Mr. W is hard of hearing and although DD had instructed the assistant to call him with warning of our impending arrival, she didn't know whether that contact had been made or, indeed, whether Mr. W was home. DD said Mr. W kept two vicious dogs in the house and she would, therefore, not enter the place in his absence.

Intent on providing us this information, she overshot the driveway. No problem; she stopped in the middle of the road and without looking in either rear view, reversed direction. A horn blared angrily, but this went unnoticed. She swung the Escort's nose hard left and we careened over the curb, sidewalk, part of the lawn and into the driveway. There we came to sort of an emotional stop - more like a pause - while DD muttered wonderings of whether he was home, whether the assistant had called and where the dogs might be. The car crept forward, two tires off the driveway crunching various small bushes and flowering plants.

At the rear of the property was a young man raking leaves. DD stopped the car and shut it down. The young man didn't know where Mr. W was and, yes, the dogs were in the house. DD suggested that we take a look around. This we did.

I made a quick circuit of the place, finishing ahead of Roberta who was stopping to look in the windows. Her presence aroused the dogs to a chorus of yipping. When she caught up to me she said, "Here I was peeking in a window and the guy was looking right at me. He's home." We told DD. With a burst of "oh mys" she went to the car, got in, cranked it up and put it into reverse, narrowly missing two trees. She jockeyed the car around until it headed down the drive, blowing the horn as she went. .

She stopped opposite the windows of the library, waving her arm out the car window and blowing the horn. Mr. W observed this from the window, motioning for us to come in. DD continued to sound the horn, waving and yelling that the dogs be "put away." After a few minutes of this, Mr. W came out of the house and said, "Why didn't you knock? Why didn't you come in?" DD replied, "Oh, I didn't know ... no lights ... afraid of the dogs. Oh, my." Assured that the dogs had been put away, DD consented to enter the house. The dogs were, in fact, spaniels of some kind that I easily managed to terrorize by growling at them.

We had barely completed the introductions when DD went flitting through the house looking something like a clumsy Loretta Young impersonator, flicking on every switch she could find, extolling the virtues of the particular room, window, staircase, floor, niche, etc. etc., in bits and pieces of disjointed dialogue as if she were a talking mockingbird. I separated myself from the tour and went off to find Mr. W. Mr. W and I were having a delightful conversation which had just veered toward how he had written a couple of textbooks during his career which continued to provide him with a modest but stable income and how he went about getting those books published, when DD swept into the room in mid sentence announcing that we had to leave. There was no retrieving the discussion with Mr. W, and it was getting late, so we said goodbye and once again embarked on some Escort *farfyghnugen*.

On the way back to the office, the conversation returned to the Sirrines, and DD discovered that we were having dinner with Anne at one of the mansions. "Oh," says DD, "I know where that is, I'll show you. I have to go by there anyway to get home. You can follow me." Fine.

So we followed her at speeds ranging from breakneck to hesitant meander along roads that I've known most of my life. In a short while, we approached the location of our dinner and DD put on her directional light. I noticed a small sign at the end of the driveway that said "Nomrah Farms." Yup, this is the place. I thought that DD would continue home. Instead, she swung into the driveway (which is about 1,000' long) and raced to its culmination in a cul-de-sac/parking area proximate to the main door. I thought she would stop. She didn't; she never hit the brakes. The vehicle fishtailed through the cul-de-sac slinging gravel. The last I saw of DD was her arm sticking out the window with its hand swiveling at the wrist in that little wave-gesture the Queen of England uses.

We went to the big front door. Anne greeted us at the door, barefoot and smiling, clad in jeans and a flowing blouse; a robust country girl juxtaposed against the background of the grand foyer. What a hoot. She showed us around the place, from the enormous kitchen to the heated swimming pool. Very nice.

Roberta's cousin Irv and his significant other (Kathy) were also dinner guests. All in all the evening was most enjoyable; warm friendly talk, a little wine, lots of laughter, a surfeit of great food (Anne is a marvelous cook).

I guess I should have figured it out for myself, but I didn't. I asked Anne who owned this place. "Nort Harmon," she said.

"Harmon?! Norton Harmon? Harmon as in Harmon Manufacturing!?"

"Yeah." Anne replied, apparently taken aback by my tone. "Nomrah is Harmon backwards."

"Well, I'll be go to hell," I said. "Ya know, 30 years ago, if Rudy, Herb and I knew the Old Man was living like this we would've burned him out. And they wonder why the peasants revolt. I'll be go to hell."

"Who are Rudy and Herb?" said Irv.

"Nobody," I replied. "Never mind."

We recently visited again with Anne at the Harmon homestead. The Harmons are in Antigua. She said that she asked Nort if he remembered me. He said, "A short, wiry guy with steel-rimmed glasses?" Anne nodded. "Yeah, I remember him. He worked the bale crew." Then, Anne said he paused, laughed and repeated, "Yeah, I remember him."

If I had ever had any second thoughts about the rat in the bale, I certainly shouldn't have. I certainly don't.

That's all I have to tell you for now. Is there any chance that you might be heading this way sometime? Also, has your finger healed sufficiently for you to dial the phone? I assume the appropriate digit is somehow indisposed, otherwise it could be used to ring me up.

Our love to you and Aunt Virginia.

College

Dear Uncle Fred,

O kay; so once again your plans have changed and I will not have the dubious privilege of gazing on your less than attractive face. I can only hope that my schedule (which is yet unpredictable, owing almost exclusively to my father-in-law's situation) will ultimately match up with yours and we will both be in New England at the same time.

I think enough time has elapsed that I might impose on your otherwise flagging capacity another inane epistle which has little, if anything at all, to do with the advancement of serious literary, intellectual, societal, cultural, political or philosophical discourse. Let me tell you up front that the genesis of the story I am about to relate was the occurrence of some difficulty in the ability of my knees to perform normal tasks, such as walking up stairs, and an insistent, throbbing pain which thwarted my desire for sleep. In my discomfort, frustration and anger, I thought of you (no offense intended) and the combination of those factors brought up a host of discordant, disconnected memories and impressions which I shall try to set in some sort of order in the following pages.

To set the context, you may recall that many years ago I managed, through flagrant stupidity, to break one knee and seriously injure the other. The legacy of that event is the frailty and attendant discomfort referred to above. I was, you may also recall (although you are forgiven if you don't recall, because I understand the synaptic dysfunction of persons of advanced age) that at that time I was in the process of being "college educated" by certain members of a monastic order.

Say what you will about those monks; that they participated in the Inquisition; that they tortured and murdered tens of thousands of people; that they stalled the development of western civilization for hundreds of years; that they terrorized and tyrannized virtually every segment of society; and that they dress funny. Yes, all true; and yet the boys know how to teach. That's why I sought their services, although I acknowledge that a financial incentive to attend had no little part in my decision.

In 1959, the then pope (a John something) initiated an "ecumenical movement," sort of a Latinesque *glasnost* or *perestroika*. A key aspect of that movement was to recognize that Catholics weren't the only Christians (or human beings) around, and maybe the world would be a better place if the western portion of it weren't so fragmented by reference to whether and which one of the scores of Christian sects one belonged to. A minor consequence of the move toward openness was what would, in the current idiot idiom, be called an "outreach program" to non-Catholic students. The specifics of that "reach"- for practical purposes - was that they encouraged non-Catholics to apply for admission and offered partial scholarships for "worthy" successful candidates (as they traditionally had for Catholics).

When I applied for admission, my brother Dave (known, for esoteric reason which I don't care to discuss, as "the Me") was about to complete his studies at junior college. My ever-hopeful and sometimes disappointed parents encouraged the Me to apply for admission "like yowuh brothuh." The sound produced by the combination (or, maybe, coagulation) of the New England/Italian accent peculiar to Rhode Island natives has always fascinated me; particularly in such, now archaic, phrases as dowah-yahd (door yard), eafs-trou (eaves-trough), izeboks (ice box), and perhaps the most musical phrase in Rhode Islandese - selluh dowah (cellar door). But I digress.

So the Me and I applied for admission and were accepted despite the fact that we listed our "religion" as "Baptist" (which, of course, we weren't really, because our father - the notorious "V man" - had taught us to think for ourselves and thus neither of us had an affiliation with any sect, Christian or otherwise).

We indicated "Baptist" for two reasons. One, because we had been exposed in our early years to the teachings of evangelical Baptists; and two, out of respect for the Brigadier, virtually the only relative we trusted in matters of the spirit.[5] Again, no offense, but you were always a cynical bastard and it would have been inappropriate under the circumstances to indicate either "none" or "cynical bastard."

We were delighted when we were told that we would be eligible for a "brothers scholarship," the conditions of which were that we were, in fact, brothers (no problem) and that we maintain at least a cumulative B average (maybe a problem). We had a penchant for doing the minimum required to pass courses. The bad habits generated by immersion in public school methods would be difficult to ameliorate in private school. If we were to maintain the scholarship (half tuition for each) I suspected that we would have to pull a bit harder on the traces.

We managed nicely for several semesters, and our cumulative average was a B. Then I broke my knee.

My injuries required that I be incarcerated in a hospital. After hours of waiting in the ER, I was manhandled by X-ray people; poked, prodded and

---

[5] Uncles Fred & Godfrey called Uncle Dave "The Brigadier." I don't remember why. Uncle Dave is a staunch Baptist; a paragon of virtue, reason and stability; a man worthy of respect.

needled by nurses; thumped and hummed over by doctors; wheeled into the solarium - there being no regular room available; and ignored for the next 24 hours. During that period Roberta visited me. She seemed quite concerned and asked about the injuries. I had no information from the medics, so I could only say, "I don't know."

Later an orderly showed up to wash the floor. He said "Hey, man, what ah you doin' heuh?" I said, "I don't know." A person I took as a nurse came in that evening and asked "Who's youh dottuh?" Now, you and I know that the English word "doctor" is derived from the Latin *docere* (to learn) from which Italian derives its *dottore* or "learned" and that the English word "doctor" doesn't mean god-like knower of all things, but simply "learned." But when someone pronounces the word as "dottuh" it sounds dumb.

In any event, I replied, "I don't know." She left. That night another patient came in to have a smoke and asked, "whattsa mattuh wit you?" I knew my line, and said, "I don't know."

The next morning, I was sitting in one of the many chairs in the solarium when a "large-boned "obviously Italian, nurse came in and said "How did you get they-uh?" I responded by reference to the patently obvious fact that I had walked.

"You cahn't do that! You have a broken knee! And why haven't yow-uh lacuhrations been soochud?" I replied, "I didn't know that, and your guess is as good as mine." She wasn't happy. She commanded that I not move a muscle and left. Within 60 seconds, two guys arrived, put me in a wheelchair and pushed me into a "treatment room" where shortly appeared a dottuh who not only soochud my lacuhrations, but also, after squinting at various X-rays, immobilized one leg from toes to hip in a plaster cast. That's what I call service.

I did not attend classes for a week or so, but the Me gave me all the assignments and fortunately I would not miss any quizzes. One of my required courses was Ethics. Of course, we're not talking modern ethics where anything can be deemed within some sort of acceptable societal standard (defined by reference to whatever subset of society suits the purpose, no matter how deviant) by rationalizing the "situation" into one of an infinite number of unique and special categories where it just so happens that anything goes. We're talking Aristotelian slash Thomistic ETHICS, where certain fixed, unquestioned (and unquestionable) standards are held to have an existence of their own in a Platonic Ideal plane of eternal, unchanging, invincible, metaphysical reality.

There is much to be said in favor of acceptance of a set of fundamental, everlasting, unquestioned, categorical propositions of human conduct. After all, if everybody in the community were to unswervingly accept such propositions, we would all be playing by the same rules. Variations from the standards could be assessed and judgments as to compliance or non-compliance would be derived with almost mathematical precision by taking the applicable proposition as a major premise, the particular conduct as a minor premise and drawing a conclusion of acceptability or non-acceptability through the use of the simple rules of formal logic.

But, of course, our community doesn't operate that way; we don't accept any such propositions. Most of us know that life is a lot messier than logic would suggest. So we just plod along, trusting that a fair number of us will conduct ourselves in a decent manner most of the time and when a breach of convention occurs such breach will be forgiven or punished depending on the significance of the breach in terms of the goals of stability, predictability and safety of the commonwealth, and how serious we are that future like breaches should be deterred.[6]

Fr. Rowe

Several of the monks taught Ethics. It was my lot, along with about 40 others, to draw Fr. Rowe. The word on Rowe was that he had been in the Navy during the war. More specifically, he had been a submariner. Word also had it that his behavior was a bit odd both in and out of the classroom. Experience would show that the word was based on fact.

Rowe and I got off on the wrong foot. In our first class meeting he announced that seating would be in reverse alphabetic order, beginning at the first row right, from his perspective. This meant that instead of taking my traditional seat somewhere in the back of the room, I would sit in the front row, directly in front of Rowe, at least as he began and ended his lecture.

At the second class meeting, Rowe began with the lord's prayer. As you know, the Catholic version of that prayer is shorter (from the Douay version of the Bible) than the same prayer as recited by Protestants (from the mighty King James version of same). With no intent of any kind, and purely from habit, I spoke the longer version ("...for Thine is the kingdom, etc.") as Rowe and the rest of the class (except Metzgar, the only Jewish guy in the class, sitting directly behind me, who didn't speak at all) went silent after "...deliver us from evil." Rowe was surprised. His mouth opened; his eyebrows went up at the center and down at the extremities.

"Well! We have a northern Christian in our midst."

[Uh-oh]

---

[6] I recognize that this and the last sentence of the prior paragraph are too long and may tax you. However, I have no desire to prolong the effort of producing this letter and have therefore opted to leave them as is. Having said that, I also recognize that I am in the process of prolonging the effort, and I'm sure you will have some sort of caustic comment in this regard.

"Mr. Villanova, isn't it?"

"Yes, sir."

"Mr. Villanova, you are apparently not of the one true faith."

"How's that, sir?"

"You're not Catholic, are you?"

"No, sir."

"What are you?"

"I'm an American. [I said this for two reasons. First, I've never thought of "what" I am in terms of religion, especially not one which is blissfully unaware of its roots in horizonal astronomy and the ancient metaphors of the killed-then-resurrected corn (or sun) god. More importantly, I suspected that this line of inquiry was heading toward perilous ground from which I hoped I could divert us. No such luck. I heard Metzgar mutter, "Oh, shit."]

"Oh, and a bit of a wise-acher, too. What's your religion, mister?"

"Baptist, sir."

"Mr. Villanova, as a Baptist, do you think it fair to waste the class' time by waiting for you to finish an unacceptable rendition of the Lord's Prayer?"

"Unacceptable to who, sir?"

"Unacceptable to **whom**; and unacceptable to the holy mother church, Mr. Villanova!"

"But, that's not my church, sir." ["Oh shit," says Metzgar]

"It is THE church. It is catholic. The word means universal. Aren't you in the universe?"

"Apparently not the same universe, sir."

"There can only be one universe, mister."

"Why must there be? Your Catholic universe isn't the same as my Baptist universe and neither is the universe of the vast majority of the other people on the planet. Are they?" ["Oh-oh-oh shit," says Metzgar]

"Sophistry and balderdash, mister, and when you address me you will call me father."

"With respect, sir, didn't Jesus say, 'call no man father'."

"Ah! The devil quotes scripture! The mother church says that I am to be called father and I will be called father!"

"That's fine with me. It's your classroom. I'll call you anything you like."

"Well thank you so much. Is there anyone else here that isn't Catholic?"

["Oh-oh-oh, shhhit," says Metzgar as he raises his hand]

"And you would be Metzgar?"

"Yes, father."

"You would be of the 'chosen people,' eh? Well let me tell you something. You boys are here because we've opened our doors to those who are not of our people. It is a matter of noblesse oblige, I suppose. Although I don't agree with it, if the Pope says we do it, then we do it. But you boys had better keep your noses clean in this classroom. That's it. I'll get on with the teaching, if the Baptist and the Jew don't have any objection." [We didn't object and he got on with it]

After class, Metzgar said, "We're dead." As he was saying that, Roncioli and St. John joined us. St. John said, "You guys are dead." I couldn't disagree. It didn't look good.

Rowe was about 40 years of age, about 6 feet tall, thin and bony. I'd say he weighed about 160 pounds. His hair was thinning and gray, cut close to his scalp. He had a long, hooked nose; a long jaw; teeth that had never been seen by an orthodontist; and bulging, blue eyes. All in all, he had the look of a madman. He never sat while he lectured. He moved around the room with quick jerky strides and gestures which, alternately accentuated and muffled by his off-white monk's robe, gave the impression of a sand hill crane engaged in an unskilled mating dance.

Rowe's teaching method was to declare the generalized proposition to be discussed during the class and for the next 45 minutes seek to apply that proposition to particularized instances, in the hope that through example we would comprehend the rule in operation and thus be capable of uniformly applying it to other like factual situations. I had, and have, no objection to this methodology.

What was missing, however, was any attempt to analyze, explain or otherwise uncover the reasons - the facts - that underpinned the rule itself. The rule was an absolute and thus impregnable. Also missing was any instance in which the rule might be suspended, deferred, modified or otherwise altered or rendered inapplicable by exception or exemption. According to Rowe, the question was solely whether the rule applied. Either it did or it didn't, and if it did then the conclusion was inexorable, unassailable and incontrovertible, regardless of the unique particulars of the situation, or as Rowe put it: whether the facts are "poopa, poopa, poopa, Father Sergent [the President of the College] or mashed potatoes." This oft-repeated chant was the summing up (his signal that he had satisfied himself, at least, that he had accomplished the QED[7]) of a pattern that went like this:

1) The rule is that all A is B
2) Now, this situation is that all B is C, and therefore
3) All C is A, and so too are all like cases, "Poopa, poopa, poopa; Father Sergent; mashed potatoes."

Rowe also illustrated what he claimed to be the "natural, fundamental, basic, god-given instinct" of all men to seek the "ultimate" (the ultimate what, I don't know) by scaling, hand over hand, a steel water pipe that ran vertically through the classroom to the room above. This display, which looked to me like a white cloaked monkey-on-a-stick, was sometimes ac-

---

[7] Abbreviation of *quod erat demonstrandum;* "which was to be demonstrated."

companied by the poopa, poopa, poopa chant. Rowe was a nut case. He had spent too long in a submerged tin can, anticipating the circumstances of death by depth charge.

Fr. Jacquard

Sometime during the prior semester Metzgar had decided that our fates were linked. I think this linkage was determined, not by any notion of karma, but by the fact that we were the only non-Catholics in our classes and he needed to feel some affinity with another alien. We had decided in that prior semester that we would take a course in Catholic theology. We were required to take a philosophy course anyway, and while we weren't required to take theology as the Catholics were, we reasoned that since we were guests at a Catholic college we could at least try to find out a little about what Catholic meant. Fr. Jacquard taught theology 1.01. We had already been linked by something neither of us was by Rowe. Jacquard soon became aware that we weren't "like" his other students, but through a different route.

Jacquard took a different approach to teaching. His approach was to state the rule, almost always a rule of Catholic dogma, then try to explain the rule by reference to history, culture, experience, policy, goals and biblical authority. In other words, Jacquard tried to demonstrate that the rule was valid based on analysis of, of all things, the facts. Facts are the only basis, and the only valid reasons, for a rule.

What tipped him off that Metzgar and I were not of the one true faith was his frequent inquiry into biblical authority. Metzgar had a grip on what Christians call the Old Testament and I had a similar hold on the New Testament. Jacquard's questions on the bible as far as the Catholic students were concerned may as well have been addressed to tree stumps. They had never read it. Striving for good grades, Metzgar and I routinely handled such questions. After several weeks of this, Jacquard asked how it came that we were the only students who could respond to his requests for information found in the Book.

"I've read it."

"And you Mr. Metzgar?"

"Just the old Book."

"You are of the Jewish faith?"

"Yes, Father. Villanova's a Baptist." [he didn't want to be alone in this]

"So that's the reason. I've got a Baptist and a Jew in my class! I should have known. You guys have the Book covered, while the rest of the class - the Catholics - sit here like a bunch of ignorant louts, unable to respond in any meaningful way to any question that isn't in the catechism. I'm left to rely on a Jew and a Baptist! What are we coming to?" [I took this as a rhetorical question. Besides, I didn't even know where "they" had been, let alone what they might be coming to. Metzgar kept whispering, "oh shit, shit, shit."]

Maybe it was a mistake to volunteer to take theology. We made Jacquard unhappy. We had no grounding to answer exam questions the way he wanted them answered (the only "right" answer is the one the professor wants). We couldn't accept the five proofs of the existence of god.

Hell, Metzgar couldn't accept Jesus Christ as an historical person, how could he accept him as the son of god? He openly expressed his total mystification with the concept of the three divine persons in one divine being. When he questioned Jacquard on this point, the good father did try to explain, but as Metzgar shook his head in uncomprehending dismay, Jacquard said,

"Look, Pete, it's like the hole in the doughnut."

"The hole in the doughnut! God is like the hole in a doughnut?"

"Metaphysically, Peter, or metaphorically, if you please. The hole doesn't exist except for the existence of the doughnut. The Holy Ghost doesn't exist without the father and the son; but since they exist, he exists."

"Who?"

"The Holy Ghost."

"I'm sorry, father. I don't get it. The hole doesn't exist. There's nothing there; otherwise, when you eat the doughnut, you'd have a hole; namely, nothing."

"I'm not talking about a doughnut, Pete."

"What are we talking about?"

"I'm trying to explain that the concept of the trinity is that the fact that two things exists creates a relationship between those two things; that relationship is also real and we call it the holy ghost."

"But suppose one or both of those things doesn't exist. There is no possible relationship then, is there?"

"Well, no. But they do."

"I don't think so." [Now, I'm saying, "oh shit."]

"Ron, you're a Christian of a sort. Can you help me out here? Haven't we established the existence of god?"

"I really wish you wouldn't ask me that, father."

"Why?"

"Because, the proofs we've discussed all suffer from a logical fallacy. They assume the point in controversy."

"Now, wait a minute. The proofs are in logical form and rest on the authority of Thomas Aquinas. What fallacy?"

"With respect to Aquinas, and to you father, I think we agree that logic proceeds from the known or the given, to the unknown; that a conclusion is valid only if it is a necessary inference from the undisputed premises; and that nothing contained in the conclusion is valid if it isn't already inherent in the premises."

"I don't need a logic lesson, Ron. Specifically, what is the fallacy?"

"Well, that the logical method is deductive only, but the proofs are essentially inductive and therefore at best lead only to a plausible - theoretical, if you will - explanation for the particulars. You can't get there from here. But I think we're getting off the track because I think Pete's difficulty is that in his tradition there is no "son" and our assertion that there is, is outside his frame of reference. Isn't that right, Pete?"

"No. [No? I'm giving you an out here you schmuck. Why are you saying no?] No, my difficulty is that I don't buy any dualist concept of divinity, Judeo-Christian or otherwise."

Jezzus sufferin' chrise, now we've had it! Whether he knew it or not (and it turns out he did) Pete had dredged up a smoldering controversy that's been going on for about 3,000 years; the reason the Aristotelians loathed and despised the Sophists; the same reason the heirs of Aristotle - the Catholic church - feared and tried to discredit and dismiss the Gnostics, Buddhists and every other "pagan" tradition; the conflict between the dualists/absolutists and the monists/relativists. Jacquard couldn't let this pass.

"That is the sin of sophistry! You Catholics pay attention. What Mr. M is saying has been banned by the church as heresy! We will have none of it. I will address this matter in detail in our next class and expose and explode the heresy Pete has suggested."

Now we were heretics. We would be lucky to get a passing grade in theology 101. I told Pete I wasn't going to open my mouth in class unless I was forced to do so and that he should take the same tact. He didn't.

The asserted "exploding" fizzled. Jacquard's exposition merely reiterated the dualist/Christian concept - borrowed from the Zoroastrians - of the conflict between the forces of light (personified in Ahura Mazda) and the forces of darkness (personified in Angra Manyu) with no attempt, and with an aversion to any attempt, to break through the metaphor and explore the unity it masks. Of course, we didn't expect any such attempt. That would have opened the possibility that good and evil (like other "pairs of opposites") are merely different faces of the same thing, and that Christ and The Devil (like their Zoroastrian counterparts) are Jungian archetypes reflected from the collective unconscious. Worse yet, that type of analysis would have raised the possibility that the dualists/absolutists had it wrong and the monists/relativists had it right.

Pete continued to challenge Catholic dogma. We both would get a C. Not good for the average.

Fr. Cain

The semester showed no sign of a happy conclusion. Not that there were no bright spots. I had the good fortune to draw Fr. Cain for symbolic logic. This was the fourth course that I had Cain (the others were cosmology, logic and rhetoric).

Cain was probably 45 at most. Like Rowe, he had been in the Navy during the war, but had served on a surface ship escorting convoys to Russia

(Mermansk, I think). All he had to worry about was being bombed or torpedoed while in waters that were cold enough to kill a man in about 2 minutes.

Cain didn't talk like a monk. He had access to the vocabulary of a sailor, and used it with infrequent, but dramatic, effect. He smoked Lucky Strikes. The bits of tobacco that periodically dislodged and stuck to his teeth or lip, he snared with his tongue and spat out.

DiTomasso did a terrific impression of Cain lecturing, smoking, searching and spitting. In fact, Cain's nickname (with affection) was "the spitter."

I think Cain enjoyed the company of the students. He was in the habit (no pun intended) of stopping in the cafeteria and joining a table of students just to chew the fat. The conversations covered topics ranging from baseball to Zen, and he spoke with confidence on all of them. Cain had his head on straight. He was a reasonable man, as comfortable listening to as leading a conversation, and sympathetic to the trivial problems the students might be having. At the time of my difficulties with Rowe, Cain and I had an open and friendly relationship in which his role was mentor.

Shortly after the event, I told Cain about Pete's kamikaze routine with Jacquard, and of my concern that, despite what I perceived as Jacquard's good nature, Pete and I were in grade trouble.

"Look, Ron, you say you're a Baptist. If being a Baptist means anything, it means that you take it as a life principle that you are a free moral agent, capable of making your own decisions. You don't need a priest class telling you what to think or what to do. Along with that freedom, you accept responsibility for your actions, good or ill. Right?"

"Well... yeah."

"All right, then. You decided to take theology. Your reasons for doing that are irrelevant at this point. You knew or should have known that you would be found out; that you would be an alien in that class; and that it was not going to be easy."

"Well... yeah."

"Well, yeah? You put yourself into the situation. Don't blame Jacquard or Metzgar. You want to see who's responsible? Look in a mirror. No one can protect anyone from the consequences of their own folly. Ron, I'm going to tell you something you won't understand now, and you might never understand. A person's situation is his own creation; a product of his beliefs, however accurate or screwed-up, about himself, his family, his friends, and whatever circumstances he thinks he perceives. Consciously or unconsciously, we all make up our own reality as we go along."

"You mean I made this all up? It's an illusion?"

"I didn't say that. I am saying that you are accountable for your own actions. Looking outside yourself and laying fault on someone else is an abdication of your individuality, your personal autonomy, your free will. And don't get hung up on "good" and "bad." Almost nothing is good or bad per se. Those are qualitative characterizations you place on things and events,

42

colored by your own belief system. Most things aren't good or bad, they just are. They only become good or bad when you try to assess them within the artificial model of reality you've constructed from your beliefs. In any event, there isn't anything so negative that it can't be viewed in some positive way. Good can come from evil."

This was pretty heady stuff for a 19 year old, country boy. Cain was right. I didn't understand what he was saying then, and I'm not sure I comprehend the full import of it some 32 years later. Now I think Fr. Cain was a closet Buddhist; and in spite of his education, training and vocation, a monist.

The Incident with Rowe

Rowe's Ethics class met three times a week; Monday, Wednesday and Friday, at 8:10 a.m. Rowe began each session with the Our Father, and glared at me while he waited for me to finish. Apparently, being a Baptist is not for sissies.

Rowe had announced at one of the early sessions that he would give homework assignments at the end of each class and that we would do those assignments in blue books that he made available for the purpose. If a blue book was handed in late for any reason, or was not handed in at all, or was incomplete, he would take one and one half points off the average of the offending student for each such book.

That was a rule.

After my stint in the hospital, I returned to classes with a full cast on my right leg, walking (sort of) with the aid of crutches. I took my place in the front row of Rowe's class, my leg sticking straight out and the crutches on the floor. Rowe took no notice. At the end of class, I put the blue books on his desk as I left the room. On the face of the first such book, I had written a note explaining that I had been in the hospital and didn't have the capacity to get the homework to him any earlier.

Next class meeting, the five blue books were slapped on the writing arm of my chair. To my note had been appended another note, in Rowe's handwriting, which said: "These are late. 7 1/2 points off your final average!" I was taken aback. Surely the good father didn't -couldn't - mean that. I would speak with him after class. After class I interrupted his departure.

"Excuse me, father. Would you have a minute?"

"What is it, Villanova?"

"It's about the blue books, father. As you can see, I've had a little accident that put me in the hospital."

"Yes. So?"

"So, I couldn't get the blue books in until Monday."

"How is that my problem?"

"It's not a problem. But 7 1/2 points off my average is a problem."

"Sounds like your problem. I told everyone very clearly that for any violation of the BLUE BOOK RULE, one and a half points would be deducted from the final average. You did hear that didn't you?"

"Yes, I did. But surely these circumstances come within an exception to the rule, or some alternate rule that forgives a person for non-compliance where circumstances beyond his control prevent his performance."

"I didn't say there was an exception. If there were exceptions, I would have said. I didn't. There are no exceptions!"

"For the love of mike, man, you're teaching ethics! Think about what you're saying."

"I know what I'm saying, and I've said it all!" [Here, he turned and began to stride away in that herky-jerky gait]

"You miserable prick!"

[He swung around; the rosary tucked into the rope belt of his robe whipped around and got stuck in the handle of his briefcase]

"WHAT? DO YOU KNOW WHO I AM?"

"I know who you are and I know WHAT you are. You're a miserable prick!"

Rowe was apoplectic. His eyes bulged fit to burst; the veins in his temples protruded; he gasped for breath as sweat beaded on his upper lip and his face mottled into a violent rose hue. I was enjoying this. He wouldn't hit a guy on crutches; would he?

"Villanova, … Villanova …I am furious [he was]. Father Jergensen will hear about this! I'll have you expelled! I'll … I'll … I'll have you EXCOMMUNICATED!"

"I'm not Catholic, sir."

"Aaugh!!"

He lurched angrily away, attempting to extract the rosary from the brief case, saying "Aaugh" and scattering astonished students from his path. What a putz.

Metzgar, Roncioli and St. John had witnessed the whole scene. St. John was hysterical, snorting "ungh-ungh-ungh" as he tried to laugh and breath at the same time. Roncioli was similarly overcome; literally banging his head against the wall. Pete wasn't laughing. He was sitting with his head in his hands, murmuring "Shit. Oh shit ... oh shit ... oh shit." "What the hell are we going to do now?" he asked through his hands. "Don't worry Pete," I said, "nothing is so negative that it can't be viewed in a positive way."

Next day my name appeared on the bulletin board as one of those miscreants who was to be brought up on charges before Fr. Jergensen, the Dean of Discipline. Fr. Cain was waiting for me near the board. "Villanova, come with me," he said. I hobbled along after him. In his office (a cubby-hole), he lit up a Lucky, dragged on it, tongue searching for that shred of leaf.

"Ron, you've screwed up. Rowe, a man mad as a hatter even in the best of circumstances [shred found, maneuvered, spat] delivered a tirade after mass this morning in which he accused you, and most of the other students, of gross misconduct, disrespect, vile and malevolent motivations and intentions, most of which are directed, so he says, at him. Now, we all know that Rowe is unstable; but in this case he does have a point. [another shred] I've talked with your buddy St. John. He tells me that you did, in fact, call Rowe a prick to his face. I suppose it is of some significance that St. John finds this so amusing, [maneuver complete - shred spat] but it is also of some significance that he corroborates Rowe's story. Do you deny that you called Fr. Rowe a prick?"

"No. I did. I was being gentle with him. He's actually a flaming, flipping asshole, and if he weren't a priest and I weren't incapacitated, I'd rip his flipping head off and piss down his neck."

"Calm down, Ron, I understand those sentiments, but I can't agree with them. This is a serious situation for you. Rowe wants you expelled. I don't want that and I've told Fr. Jergensen I don't want that. But Fr. Sergent knows about the incident and, while he is sympathetic, he can't just let this pass. We've got to live with this guy whether you're here or not here. What do you want?"

"Look, father, I don't deserve to have my average reduced by 7 1/2 points. What kind of bullshit is that? I did everything I could do. Rowe has it in for me because I'm not Catholic, I say a different version of the lord's prayer, and probably because I'm of Italian ancestry. Say what you want to defend him, but the guy's a 14-carat asshole. What do I want? I want out of his classroom, which is what he wants too."

"All that aside, Ron, you did call a priest a prick. Whatever else he might be, he earned his stripes and you can't be insubordinate with impunity. There's going to be a price to pay. I'll talk with Jergensen and Sergent, but I can't promise anything."

I thanked Cain for whatever help he might be able to lend me. My hearing with Jergensen was later that day. At the designated hour I went in to the Office of the Dean of Discipline. Jergensen was in the anteroom.

"Hi, Ron. Come on in. [I did] Have a seat. Geez, I didn't know you were on crutches. Broken leg?"

"Knee, actually."

"Sounds nasty. I hope you don't have any permanent disability."

"Thanks. I hope not."

"Tell me. Ron, just what went on the other day with Fr. Rowe?" [I told him my version of the story, indicating the peculiar injustice of my treatment at the hands of a man of god who was supposedly an expert on the subject of ethics. I freely acknowledged that I had used the offending words, and that I was not remorseful for their use]

"Fr. Cain speaks very highly of you, Ron. Your scholastic record is excellent, and your other professors have nothing but positive things to say. I know you're married and I know you work full time. I'm inclined, and Fr. Sergent agrees, to write this off to a 'heat of the moment' outburst that won't happen again. Am I safe in taking that position?"

"Yes, sir."

"Good. However, some form of penalty must be exacted. Fr. Cain feels that the most appropriate penalty is to not allow you to have what you want. He says that would be too easy. I agree. We have, therefore, decided that you will remain in Fr. Rowe's class. To me, that is a severe penalty. What do you think?" [At that point I thought Cain was my best friend and my worst enemy. Talk about making a point.]

"I think it's going to be a nightmare."

"Good, good, good! So be it. I'll talk to Rowe. I think I can persuade him that this is best for both of you. Don't worry about flunking. That's not going to happen, but you'd better ace a couple of your other courses if you want to keep that scholarship. You're dismissed. [I started to leave] And, ... oh yeah. Ron, ... you really shouldn't have called the man a prick … even if he is."

It was a nightmare. Pete and I were silent for the rest of the semester. The other members of the class acted as if there was a UXB in the room.[8] We took the maximum number of permissible cuts. We did the best we could on the final exam. Pete got a C; I got a D. Whether deserved or not, I don't know, but Cain gave me an A in symbolic logic, and I was awarded an A in both English lit. (medieval) and metaphysics. The Me understood the pressure, sucked it up, and carried more than his full share of the load. We made a cumulative B.

Cain acknowledged that it was his idea to keep me in Rowe's class. He said it would do both our souls some good if we didn't just walk away from the conflict, but saw it through. He said he wasn't about to be an "instrument of interference" with our karmas; that Rowe and I had had this run-in for a reason. He didn't know the reason, but was sure that there was one, and in the long run it would be a positive factor to serve our time together, three hours a week for about three months. I wonder whether he understood the short-term effect of his idea.

He probably knew that there would be future effects from the D in Ethics, and there were some. When I went for the required interview prior to my acceptance at law school, the first question out of the mouth of the interviewer was "You were graduated cum laude from college. What's this D in Ethics about?" I explained without mincing words.

Ethics of a different sort is taught in law school (for all the good it does). I took the law school ethics course in the last semester of my final year. I didn't buy the book. I attended the first class and the last class. My friend, Bill, asked me: "Villanova, how do you intend to pass this course? You haven't showed up; you don't even have the book." "Bill," I said, "if I can't

---

[8] Unexploded bomb

pass this course by the seat of my pants, I don't deserve to graduate law school." I took the exam. I was awarded an A. I figure the two grades average out to about a B.

I don't know what happened to Rowe. I can't say that I care. He's probably dead by now. Outliving people like that is some measure of perverse satisfaction. I don't know what became of Metzgar, St. John or Roncioli either. The latter two were accepted at BC law. I wonder how they did in ethics.

That's the story. I'll let you go do something enjoyable now. Try to take care of yourself and Aunt Virginia. I do hope to see you soon. And, yeah, by the way, it wouldn't kill you to put a pen to paper and bore me with some of your outlandish stories.

Love to you and Aunt Virginia.

Burying Old John

Dear Uncle Fred

I was just drafting a will for Aunt Hilda (a topic we discussed during our most recent telephone conversation, but which you have probably already forgotten), and when I finished I discovered that my spouse is thoroughly engrossed in "her" soap opera. I've, therefore, taken the opportunity to switch files and begin this missal.

Roberta reviews and critiques all my correspondence before it is sent. Her comment on my last letter was that I hadn't given you much news. I responded that I had given you as much as I thought a reasonable man could tolerate in one sitting and that I would fill you in on other happenings at some future point. I guess this is "some future point" so I'll give you a bit more now, though I must be selective because there are so many events I could report that it would produce a small, but thoroughly dull and irretrievably dreary, book.

Let me tell you about burying "Old John." Old John is (or rather, was) Roberta's natural (biological) father. I don't know much about the man. I met him twice; he wasn't a guy I wanted to be around. My information is that my assessment of him was not unique; rather it was an opinion shared by his friends, family and associates. Not that Roberta knew him much better than I. She had seen him perhaps a half dozen times over a period of 35 years. Old John lived in an ancient house in the woods, eking out a subsistence living by house painting whenever his addiction to alcohol would either allow or demand

49

that activity. He also "lived off the land," which essentially translates into: he shot a few rabbits or a deer once in a while, and raised some chickens.

About three years ago, a drinking buddy found Old John in his favorite (read, only) chair, stone cold dead. Cause of death was dutifully noted on the death certificate as "alcoholism." Roberta was notified of this unhappy event by her (to that point virtually unknown) Uncle Fred, brother of the deceased, who informed her that she should participate in or, indeed, direct the funeral arrangements. I believe (though it turns out Fred is a decent fellow) that the bereaved family was as much interested in shifting whatever financial burden might be incurred by the necessary burial, et cetera, as it was in allowing the child of the decedent to have a hand in the arrangements. To no one's surprise the old man died, not only penniless but, in debt.

Roberta handled the funeral arrangements, trying to satisfy the needs, wants and desires of the various factions of varying sentiment within the family. It is, I suppose, never possible to satisfy everyone, but she did a good job of balancing the competing interests and wants (i.e., there were no fistfights at the wake). The old man was laid out in his favorite fishing attire, complete with hat; people remarked how natural he looked (this despite the absence of a beer - or other - bottle in his hand).

My first ever visit to Old John's house was shortly after the funeral. We were not the first to get to the house, as was evident from the disappearance of certain articles thought valuable in that part of the woods; e.g., shotguns and chain saws.

What was left after the late night visits of the neighbors was a collection of "stuff" that had been gathering for decades, virtually none of it worth much of anything to anyone other than the Salvation Army. The condition of the place was, to put it mildly, poor. The house was home to several dogs, a dozen cats, numerous chickens and a couple of goats. The crowning touch was in the cellar: the carcass of a deer that had been left hanging for about six months. My sons Robert and Dean had assisted at the funeral by helping me (and others) carry the casket. They joined us at the house. Robert and Dean are accomplished craftsmen, familiar through experience with old houses and the renovation of same.

Standing outside the house (it was virtually impossible to stay within the structure because of the mingled odor of excrement from the various living animals and the stench of the dead one in the cellar) I said to Dean, "what would it take to rehab this place?" This was more a rhetorical question than a serious inquiry. Dean didn't hesitate a nanosecond, responding, "Get a bulldozer, push it into the cellar hole. Build somewhere else." Roberta determined then and there that if she were to participate in a distribution of the Old Man's estate, she would relinquish any claim that she might have on the house. I concurred.

A popular question was whether Old John had left a will. The common expectation among those who gathered at the wake was that he would have left his estate to the boy scouts (something he had said infrequently) or that he would leave it to his estranged significant other. To the surprise and shock of some, and to the shock and delight of others, the old man hadn't left a will. In this state that means that the estate is to be divided equally among the surviving children, in this case, Roberta and her brother, Sonny.

The funeral director, who alleged that he was a good friend of Old John and knew what the old man would have wanted (strange how so many people become mind readers after the mind to be read becomes worm food) suggested that Roberta donate some land to the Boy Scouts, asserting also that this would be a good tax avoidance device. When that suggestion met nothing but silence, he switched to "You'll probably have to get rid of some of the property just to pay the taxes anyway." We said nothing to indicate to him that he was a fool for even suggesting such a thing, and that we would be greater fools if we took the suggestion. Besides, at this point we didn't know whether there was an estate worth worrying about or whether Roberta would become an heiress.

In the opinion of Old John's brother, Herb, "Those kids should get everything, and that would be right. The man never gave those kids nothin'. Why, he didn't draw a sober breath for the last four years. Never gave those kids a thought. Serve him right that the kids get it." Thanks for the thoughts Uncle Herby.

A something less than diligent search of the house did not turn up anything that resembled a will. We knew that Old John had been involved in a virtual plethora of legal (quasi-criminal) scrapes over the years and had used a local attorney named Vasile Tapodis to help him stay out of jail. It seemed prudent to inquire of Vasile whether he had ever drafted or had knowledge of a possible will. This we did. Vasile had never made a will for Old John and his query to other local attorneys disclosed no such document.

The laws of intestacy appeared to apply, so it became appropriate to determine just what the estate might be. Sonny insisted on using Vasile to handle the estate (since Sonny, like Old John, was in the habit of using Vasile to aid him in subverting the legal process by keeping Sonny out of jail, which in his case did not always succeed). I didn't trust Vasile to handle a jaywalking citation but, to keep the peace, Roberta consented to putting Vasile on the case.

In brief, the estate was approximately 94 acres of land, including the ramshackle house sitting on it. To our amazement, no liens or mortgages were attached to the property, and the old man's indebtedness was something less than $5,000. Suddenly it appeared that Roberta was a land Baroness. But wait, there's always a price to be paid, and that maxim was to apply with great vigor in this situation. To put this aspect of the story into perspective it is necessary to interrupt the (more or less) chronological flow and enter into a brief digression.

Sonny is the product of a mix of a dubious genetic inheritance and an unfortunate absence of nurturing. I don't want to get into a debate about the pros and cons of nature versus nurture; suffice it to say that this lad (now aged almost 50 years) got something toward the short end of both. This is not to say that he is a bad person; he does have his moments, many people find him charming in a rustic sort of way, and he often shows his feelings in a way that belies his otherwise bellicose, macho bullshit persona. I think one incident will serve as an illustration of that persona.

Several years ago, he agreed to prepare Thanksgiving dinner for his significant other (Sherry, the mother of one of Sonny's six or seven children, and the woman he has lived with for many years but doesn't see fit to marry, something he had tried - like Old John - twice before with disastrous results).[9] Sonny likes to cook, does it well, and takes a great deal of pride in preparing such a multi-course festive array as is traditional for the holiday.

Sherry decided to visit with her mother for a while. Sonny happily consented to that absence because he didn't want her lurking around the kitchen while he was working; but admonished her to be back by 2 o'clock. Dinner guests arrived at about 1:45 and were treated to the smells of the kitchen and a healthy dose of an alcoholic beverage, Sonny participating in the libation. The guests were a young man that sometimes worked with Sonny during his infrequent forays into the world of labor, and a young woman who did not know Sonny other than by his somewhat disreputable reputation. At 2 o'clock Sherry was not home; Sonny had a drink.

---

[9] Don't get confused. This is not the tattooed Sherry at the Johnson house. This Sherry is a good person, and we are quite fond of her.

At 2:15 Sherry was not home; Sonny had a drink; ditto 2:30, 2:40, 2:47, 2:54 and 3:00.

When 3:15 came around, with Sherry yet in absentia, Sonny was in a state of irrepressible, alcohol abetted, clamorous fury. Not having the primary object of his wrath available for confrontation, he did the only thing he could do. Pulling his 38 Smith & Wesson from its convenient location in a kitchen drawer he denounced Sherry for her insensitive and reprehensible disregard for his instruction, his sensibilities and his beneficence, her wanton cruelty toward the guests, and with wild gestures and profane language declared the holiday at an end, kicked open the oven door and declaring, "It's over, it's over, it's over!!" discharged the contents of the revolver into the turkey. The guests were astonished and horrified.

The young lady in particular seemed to interpret this display as somehow threatening, as evidenced by her precipitous flight from the house. Her fear and amazement remained unabated, however. She escaped to the refuge of a neighbor's house, and from there called the police, who arrived promptly, assayed the situation and arrested Sonny on various charges including risk of injury to a minor; disturbing the peace; discharging a firearm within the town limits; breach of the Wildlife Preservation Act of 1963, as amended; and violation of the Anti-Cruelty to Animals Act of 1898, Section 14-67(b)(2)(ii), as amended by Public Act 44-204.

Justice here can move swiftly. By 9:30 on Monday, Sonny was brought before Judge Hiram Smeed by a representative of the State Attorney's Office. Also present at that time were approximately 30 other miscreants, mostly traffic law violators, who upon the reading of the charges (a necessary part of criminal proceedings) against Sonny, fell to a man into such a raucous burst of commentary and laughter that the judge found it necessary to threaten to clear the chamber and hold everyone in contempt to restore order.

When an uneasy order was restored, the judge asked counsel and the accused to approach the bench. Judge Smeed had the look of a man who had begun his day in need of Pepto Bismol, his bloated red face contained two small, watery eyes that were trying to recede into his sinuses while his eyebrows sent errant sprouts of mutant follicles in search of his ears. Not a man to be trifled with. "Tell me, Sir," he said in a surprisingly dispassionate, almost fatherly, voice, "what did you do?"

"I shot the bird, " says Sonny.

A pregnant silence. Then – uproar. Pandemonium explodes. Laughter, hooting, choking; a young woman with a front tooth missing puts her hands to her face, tears slinking down her checks, mock shoot-outs followed by impressions of dying turkey gobbles, the bailiff turns his face to the wall. The judge sees no humor in the situation. He jumps to his feet, gavel in hand, hammering the bench "Order! Order! I will have order!" But there is no order. "Bailiff, clear the court, there will be a ten minute recess," Smeed declares as he, in disgust, leaves the bench for his chambers.

It took 15 minutes to control, then clear, the court. Recess lasted 25 minutes and when court resumed Smeed, the bailiff, the State's Attorney and Sonny had the courtroom to themselves. Smeed began,

"I have considered the facts [read, I just read the file] in this case, and in order that this bit of nonsense not further disrupt my court, I am prepared to resolve it. I am not prepared to say that you have not done something wrong, but I am also not prepared to say that whatever it is you have done wrong is punishable by the State. It has never come to my attention, nor can the State seriously contend, that shooting a dead animal is an offense against some statutory prohibition. Nor can I find that the young woman who initiated this ruckus was ever threatened or at risk (especially since she has declined to pursue such claims). Further, while it is clear that you did discharge a firearm within the town limits, it is also true that the said discharge was within the confines of your home. This is, for this court at least, a case of first impression and as such I have it within my discretion to make a determination based upon general principles of law and of the general standards of society.

The court is aware of the ever-increasing encroachment by the government on the activities of its citizens. It can be said with little exaggeration that about the only thing a citizen might do without provoking the full prosecutorial apparatus of the state is to walk calmly down the center of the sidewalk, looking neither left nor right, speaking to no one and breathing unobtrusively through his nose. Be that as it may, the distinction I wish to draw is between conduct in public and conduct within the privacy of one's home. Surely, the scope of the state's interest must stop somewhere, and I have chosen in this case to have it stop at your front door.

What combination of extraordinary circumstances induced you to discharge a weapon into a turkey, I do not know and, moreover, I do not want to know. Suffice it to say that as far as I am concerned you may shoot up the entire contents of your kitchen without let or hindrance from this court. The charges are dismissed and you are directed to remain silent as you remove yourself immediately from my presence."

Justice, American style.

Sonny was in fact one of Old John's drinking buddies and the boys often got up to mischief together (you know, that adolescent male bonding crap). The result was that Sonny was "close" to his father. Roberta (being a nondrinker and a mature, responsible adult) was not. Sonny perceived this "closeness" as bestowing on him a sort of supremacy (an unwarranted, chauvinistic, maleness thing) with respect to the control and disposition of Old John's estate. Roberta did not share this perception, but out of unwarranted kindness toward her brother (I could tell you "poor Sonny" stories) decided to allow him to think that he had such power. So now I've come back to putting Vasile on the case.

About a month after the funeral, Roberta received a letter from Vasile enclosing a probate court form that purported to appoint Sonny as administrator of the estate. When the substance of the form and its portent of possible future events had been considered for all of 30 seconds, Roberta was on the phone to Vasile. She advised him, in crisp, concise and precise words and phrases, that she was to be named co-administrator. If I were on the other end of the line, the tone and tenor of the advice would have been sufficient to alert me that I was not dealing with your "ordinary bear." But as events would show, Vasile was not as perceptive as he might have been.

In time, the probate court issued letters testamentary (as we call them) appointing Sonny and Roberta as co-administrators. The next step in the process was the filing of the inventory of the estate. As I said, the estate consisted of some personal property of relatively little value and the real estate, the latter to be valued by independent appraisal for estate tax purposes. Vasile had come up with the inventory and asked that Roberta trek up to his office on a Saturday morning, saying that "I need to discuss a few things with you." I surmised that what he wanted to discuss was "the matter of my fee." Roberta asked that I join her in this foray; I agreed.

The office was in a little New England town with a population of about 2,000 people. Like so many other towns in the eastern part of the state, it was at one time owned and controlled by a textile mill. The mill still stands, but its only use now is storage and the housing of a plumbing supply wholesaler. Whatever vitality the town might have had disappeared when the mill owners decided to relocate operations to warmer climes, and cheaper labor, down south. The place has the look of age. In spite of some fresh paint on Main Street, the feel of decay sits on everything. Vasile's office had fresh paint.

A person who introduced herself as Vasile's sister greeted us. A woman of about 60 years of age, she had a brusque manner and a face that looked like it had been used to split wood. She directed us to wait in the conference room; which we did. Vasile arrived shortly thereafter; introduced himself and sat down. I did the honors for the Villanova team. Sister hatchet face joined us. There was no offer of coffee. Vasile began,

"Roberta, you know that I've been working on the inventory for your father's estate. The only thing of real value is the land. Since he didn't have a will, the law is that you and your brother share equally. Now, I know your brother, I've done some work for him and, of course, I did some work for your father too. The land does have considerable value. That's good. But it's also a problem because to settle the estate, taxes have to be paid. The property has been appraised at $3,000 per acre. I suggest that you sell some of the property to pay the taxes."

Now, I'm just a country boy, but I know what I know; and I know the smell of a rat. Roberta and I had never had any truck with any of the characters involved in this story. They didn't know us. But we had done our homework. Roberta has experience with and an understanding of real estate. She had spoken and visited with the man who had appraised the property. She knew that an appraisal for estate tax purposes is one thing, and that market value is another.

She also knew that of the 94 acres, about 20 was currently marketable and that those 20 could be split into four house lots with a market value (even in the then depressed market) of about $40,000 per parcel. Obviously, the appraised value was an average for all the acreage, and didn't differentiate between those parts that had road frontage and those that were almost inaccessible. We will never know, but both Roberta and I immediately assumed that Vasile had some crony waiting in the wings ready to offer her $3,000 per acre for "as many acres as she was willing to part with, upon the advice of her counsel." We looked at each other. I got the message.

I asked what the amount of the taxes might be. Vasile advised me that the taxes were set out in the statute and that he thought they would run around $21,000. I went for some specificity, "Isn't it more like $19,000?" "Well, I'd have to look it up," he replied. "Don't bother" I said, "I already have; the amount is about $19,000. But whatever it is, there's no need to sell any land. Roberta and I will take care of the estate's expenses." Vasile and sister looked at each other with expressions of mixed surprise, consternation and (I think) disappointment. They hadn't planned on this. The expectation of a quick and painless profit by the manipulation, under the guise of help, of a couple of yokels had been dashed by a few unanticipated words.

Sister couldn't contain herself. "What did you say you did for a living?" said she. "I didn't," said I, "but now that you ask, I'm an attorney." "Oh," she said. "I didn't know that," said Vasile, "where do you practice?" I told him. "What's you specialty?" "Tax and securities, and Roberta is the President of PKL, Inc. and RCV Realty," I answered.

They knew the jig was up. It was time to forget the condescension and to change tactics. "Well, if the expenses won't be a problem, how would you suggest we proceed?" said Vasile. Clearly he had not prepared for this contingency and was concerned lest he misstep again. "Roberta and I have discussed this in some detail," I said, "and with her permission I will tell you what she proposes as a fair and equitable distribution of the estate." Receiving the go ahead from Roberta and Vasile I explained that since Sonny had no home of his own and wanted his father's house, Roberta wanted her brother to have the house; and since she would be paying the estate expenses, the land should be divided in such a way that Sonny would have the house and some acreage around it. Roberta should have that number of acres determined by a formula which recognizes the grant of her half interest in the house to her brother and also recognizes that she will pay Sonny's half of the estate expenses, using the per acre valuation as determined for probate purposes.

This explanation seemed a bit much for the pair across the table. After a period of silence, Vasile asked that I write up the proposal. I agreed, not only because I wanted it to be in writing, but because I discerned that that would be the only way to make sure Vasile understood it.

Writing up the proposal proved to be the easy part. Persuading Sonny was quite another matter. The property consisted of about 74 acres north of Pond Rd., with the house located toward the West side. A brook marks the western boundary of the property. The other 20 acres is South of the road. It terminates to the South in the middle of the pond, and to the East and West by the said brook which flows into the pond at its westerly end and exits over a rude dam at its easterly end. North of the road there exists a gravel bank with a particularly good grade of sand and gravel deposited after the retreat of the glacier which covered New England during the last ice age. A geology professor from the University of Connecticut takes one of his classes to the site each year to show them an example of an interesting, geologically at least, terminal moraine. The pond itself is not very large, but it is very attractive and is stocked with trout each year by the state wildlife folks. The land south of the road abuts both the road and the pond, and is therefore, of greater value than the remainder of the property.

Roberta consulted the real estate appraiser who had done the probate valuation (a man named Pratt) as to how the land could be reasonably divided. Pratt had no hesitation in suggesting that all the land around the pond and another 35 or so acres north of the road that includes the gravel bank, should go to Roberta. His reasoning was simple: the land around the pond is more valuable; the gravel bank has value; and she would end up with approximately 2100 feet of frontage out of a total of 2800. That, I think, struck Roberta as a bit overreaching, but it was one way of doing it.

Roberta and I walked the property shortly after her meeting with Pratt. We were both particularly impressed with the Western side of the property because it was more level than the Eastern side, nicely wooded, and quite beautiful along the brook. This fact, and the fact that Roberta was sensitive and sympathetic to her brother's desire to have at least a share of the property around the pond, and a source of income from the gravel bank, led her to develop two other methods of dividing the land, both of which were more favorable to Sonny, and one of which was very generous. We drew up the three versions of a distribution and went up to the house (in which Sonny had ensconced himself the day after the funeral) to discuss the options with Sonny.

There wasn't much discussion. Sonny did not want a discussion. He didn't want to talk about it. He couldn't talk about it. He didn't want to divide up Old John's legacy. He just knew Old John would roll over in his grave; Old John wants to keep the property together and never let it get out of the family. There were intimations of (what I thought was the discredited doctrine of) primogeniture. We were going nowhere; and we went nowhere for more than six months.

During that time there were several telephone calls from a besotted brother-in-law, barely intelligible, disjointed and rambling, the purpose of which was to offer counter proposals that I was to pass on to Roberta. These were so nonsensical that I couldn't understand them and I, thus, can't recall the details.

One ran like this (I think): Sonny would sell off some of the land (Roberta's) in order to obtain the money to buyout Roberta. I advised him that I would pass this on to her, but I did not think she would be very keen on the idea, since she already had a legal right to one-half of the estate and intended to be reimbursed in some manner for her payment of estate expenses that were rightfully his burden. I did. She wasn't.

Fearful lest I be missing something serious in this scheme, I told Dean about the proposal. He thought for a moment, then said, "You know that $500 I owe you, Pop? What I'll do is this: I'll sell your boat and pay you back." Case closed.

I should also tell you, just to give you some of the flavor of this experience, that Dean happened to pick up the phone on one of the occasions that Sonny had muddled his mind with alcohol and fixed to converse with me. Good kid that he is, he told his Uncle I wasn't home. There ensued another lengthy and confused conversation after ten minutes of which Sonny said:

"Ronnie .... Ronnie .... don't bullshit me now. I know what you're doin'. All you lawyers and judges do it. You're snortin' coke, aren't ya. Don't bullshit me Ronnie, I know you're doin' it. You're high as a kite right now. You don't even sound like you!"

Dean was surprised and amused (he knows his uncle) and replied

"Uncle, this is Dean; you know, your nephew Dean, Ronnie's son Dean."
Then he heard

"OH OH, Deano, that's you Deano, my nephew Deano. You're my favorite nephew ya' know. No wonder you didn't sound like you."

The scary thing is that my children played in the same gene pool lottery as their uncle. Thank god they lost.

Anyway, time went on with no result. Good that I am a patient man (NOT!). Roberta had informed her brother that she would be willing (indeed she told him outright that what she wanted was) to take the westerly and northerly acreage of the property (thus giving herself 700 feet of frontage and the least valuable acres) and that he could take the piece, including the house, which contained the gravel bank and the pond (this was the most generous offer that could have been made under the circumstances). I expected (perhaps because I am a reasonable man and assume that same reasonableness in others - incorrectly, of course) that Sonny would jump at the opportunity. I felt that Roberta was really giving herself the short end of the stick.

I was, therefore, unprepared when Roberta told me that Sonny had indicated a reluctance to accept that proposal and had expressed interest in claiming that parcel that Roberta had been willing to accept. My only explanation for such a desire on Sonny's part is that he thought Roberta was "using psychology" on him, and that the parcel she had picked must be of greater value if she wanted it; therefore, he wanted it.

After more time passed, Roberta made an appointment with her brother for a meeting on Sunday at 12 o'clock, the rationale being that Sonny would probably not have enough time on Sunday morning to become inebriated to the point of incompetence or incoherence. We arrived at the appointed hour to find Sonny semi-sober. After what seemed like too much pointless conversation, Sonny determined that we should "tour the property" by riding in a cart which he had fabricated and attached to an ancient John Deere tractor. The tractor was part of Old John's legacy and hadn't run in a decade, but Sonny is an excellent mechanic and in calm moments can fix just about anything that is fixable.

Roberta and Sherry were disinclined to journey behind the tractor, but rather than give excuse for the creation of yet another scene, they permitted themselves to be dragooned.

As I said, the tractor was ancient and, like all tractors, exceedingly slow, particularly in the rough, wooded, and rocky terrain that we proceeded to cover. Sonny had brought along a six-pack of his favorite and carried on a tediously detailed and almost comical commentary with respect to virtually each tree, boulder and bush that we inched by. He stopped often to point out features of particular interest or curiosity, and stopped often to relieve himself of the burden that the continuous ingestion of mead was putting on his kidneys. About two hours into the excursion we found ourselves at the westerly side of the property, near the brook.

The sylvan glade that Roberta and I remembered had vanished. It had vanished by operation of its conversion into a dumping ground for most of the debris which had previously occupied the house and its yard, and all the debris and household garbage that Sonny & company had produced since they moved in. There were piles of biodegradable and non-biodegradable refuse and human detritus scattered over an area of two to three acres; the crowning blight being a row (more or less) of eight partially cannibalized vehicles (seven old Fords and one Datsun) which Sonny deemed to have value and had dragged to this spot for perpetual outside storage.

It was at this spot that Sonny, now full eloquent as the fifth in the six-pack passed his gullet, gave his ode to the wilderness oration. Standing on the tractor, his outstretched arm waving the fifth of the six pack round all the cardinal points, praised the trees, their leaves; the bushes, their berries; the birds, their song; the sky, its blue; the water, its sparkle; etc., etc. *ad nauseum.* He proclaimed his intent to one day build with his own hands and with the fruits of the forest itself, a log cabin on this spot (a window toward the dump?), where he and his family (which one?) would live idyllically amidst the glory of the forest and the ever present gurgling of the brook.

Include me out.

It took another hour to get back to the house. By that time we had to get back; the sixth of the six-pack had passed through to its inevitable absorption into the forest floor. Roberta was beyond conversation. Sonny was incapable of it. I wanted to be gone as quickly as possible. We made our escape. As we started home, Roberta said, "Get me out of here. I don't care what he wants. Whatever he wants he can have. I want it to be over."

Easier said than done.

What had transpired was essentially this. That day's experience had shown us the futility of trying to help someone who doesn't want to be helped. Roberta had thought, for example, that if Sonny had his own home, he would feel more secure, more like he had some permanence, more like he had a stake in conducting himself in a more responsible, socially acceptable, manner. She had also thought that the kind, considerate, sisterly thing to do in view of her economic situation *vis a vis* his, was to let him have the better part of the estate; he could sell gravel and, if need be, (and in was my opinion that there probably would be a need) he could sell those pieces of property which fronted the road.

She now gave up on trying to be generous. If Sonny wanted the least attractive option, and he wanted to use it as a dump - fine, so be it.

Once again I wrote to Vasile, specifying in detail the (apparent) agreement that the siblings had reached. I drew him a map; drew in the lines; used different colors to distinguish Roberta's parcel from Sonny's parcel; indicated boundaries and the number of feet between points. I instructed Vasile to draw up a mutual distribution agreement that could be presented to the probate court for its approval, suggested what such a document might say, and recommended that the description of property be based upon the existing deed so that a new survey would not be needed. I also told him to send a draft of the document to me and advised him that if the draft were acceptable to Roberta, it would be his job to get Sonny into his office to sign the final document (this last was my attempt to get him to do something to earn his fee).

More time passed. There were more strange conversations, but it appeared that the agreement would hold. Sonny lamented the division of the land. He couldn't bring himself to sign anything. Dad would be upset. More time passed. The document was put into final form and sent to Sonny. More time passed.

About two and a half years after the demise of Old John, his estate had not yet been settled. There were difficulties with the town tax collector. It seems that because Roberta's name appeared on all the checks that had been used to pay estate expenses, including town taxes, the town assumed that Roberta would be paying the taxes on the house and on the motor vehicles that her brother had on the property. Now, assuming that Roberta would be paying all the freight for her brother is one thing, after all it could look like that to someone who was simply observing the various transactions, but then something happened which went entirely too far.

An envelope addressed to me from the Town Tax Collector showed up in the mailbox. The contents of the envelope asserted that I, Ronald Villanova, was now delinquent on my debt to the Town; to wit, that I had failed to pay the appropriate taxes assessed against certain specified motor vehicles and land, and that in the absence of prompt payment, action would be taken to attach or otherwise secure liens against whatever property of mine the sheriff might find within the State.

Now, certainly anyone who has been married for a number of years understands full well that marriage is more than a union with another person. There is truth in the old saw that you not only marry your spouse, but the spouse's family as well. Most spouses know that it is necessary to do many things that he or she might not want to do in order to accommodate the multiple relationships that exist prior to marriage and continue thereafter. Marriage carries the burden of familial luggage that is otherwise wholly external to the relationship between the spouses. Even under the best of circumstances (e.g., where one actually likes and gets along with one's in-laws, and they reciprocate) those external burdens can sometimes put strains on the spousal relationship. Such strains increase by orders of magnitude where the best of circumstances do not exist and the obverse pertains.

If you have been paying any attention at all to this little story, you must have discerned that I perceive the familial luggage as coming within the obverse category of the "best circumstances" coin. This has nothing to do with Roberta who, if she were Catholic, would have already been beatified for her unstinting (and largely unappreciated and misunderstood) efforts to maintain some sort of bond of mutual concern and affection with her brother (and her mother - a story of its own, which would require a very long dissertation to fathom). I do not share her empathy for the individuals who comprise her original family. I have learned through long, unpleasant experience that the game simply isn't worth the candle.

I realize that this failure of concern reveals a personality flaw; i.e., that I am self- centered, self-absorbed and don't really give two straws for other peoples' feelings or problems; but there you have it. I am what I am, and that's all what I am (to quote that existential philosopher - Popeye).

I have long accommodated my spouse's family and its idiosyncrasies. Not for their sake, but for hers. However, there comes a time when a line must be drawn. I suppose we could argue for years about where the line should be drawn and why it should be drawn in one place rather than another, and what exceptions and qualifications should be placed on such line drawing. When I read the notice from the Tax Collector, however, there was no thought of debate; this was far enough; my patience (if I ever had any) was at an end. I telephoned Roberta (she was in Florida at the time) to inform her of the latest event and to make my position known. The conversation went something like this:

"Hello

"Hi, how you doing?"

"Oh, fine: it's hot. What's new up there?"

"Funny you should ask. I got some mail today that I think is misdirected."

"Oh? What is it?"

"It's a notice from the Tax Collector that if I don't pay your brother's taxes they're going to put a lien on our house, that's what it is."

"Huh? What the hell is that about?"

"I'm not sure; but I am sure that I'm not going to put up with this bullshit. Fa Chrise sake, isn't it enough that we paid to bury your grandmother, and your aunt, and now your father? Isn't it enough that we've paid your father's bills and your brother's share of the probate expenses? It would be one thing if they sent this notice to you, but they sent it to me. The notice is made out to me fa Chrise sake! I've goddam had it! This is bullshit. *Basta e basta!*"[10]

"Ronald, you're ranting. Calm down."

"I'm not goddam ranting!"

"Yes, you are. You're using Italian."

"Porcho della miseria, I'm not goddam ranting and I'm not using Italian."[11]

"Yes you are. Whenever you rant you revert to your childhood and use all those negative, semi-obscene Italian phrases your uncles taught you."

"They never did."

"They always did."

"Who are 'they' that always did?"

"Your uncles."

"Which uncles?"

"All of them."

"That isn't true. You can't make a flat-out universal affirmative statement like that."

"Yes I can. I did. It is true, and you are ranting. That's because you're emotionally immature. It's your fundamental nature that expresses itself in a childish tantrum whenever something, no matter how trivial, upsets you."

"Non sei cosi bruto con me, bambina![12] It isn't trivial, and don't lay that psychology bullshit on me!"

"See, that's just what I mean. Now, calm down, and tell me what it is you think I can do about this from 1250 miles away."

I hate it when she nails me like that. She was, as always, right (that's why I hate it). I was ranting. There was nothing she could do about it. I guess I

---

[10] Enough is enough

[11] Miserable pig

[12] Don't be so ugly with me.

just needed someone to rant to. But like I said, it was time to draw a line; and I knew just the person I was going to draw the line on. I called Vasile. That conversation went something like this:

"Hello, is Vasile available?"

"Yeah, hold on." [It was hatchet-face who answered the phone. She has a delightful manner, eh?]

"Hello."

"Yeah, Vasile [tact was no longer to be utilized] this is Ron. You know, the guy who pays the bills?"

"Oh, hi Ron."

"Yeah, look, Vasile, I got another bill in front of me here, only this one has a twist; it's made out to me and threatens attachment of my assets."

"Oh, gee, that can't be right."

"Damn straight it can't be right. I think this has gone far enough. First thing you're gonna do is call the Tax Collector and tell them they screwed up and that this bill goes to Sonny. Next thing you're gonna do is petition the probate court for a partition of the property in accordance with the agreement that Roberta and John reached. If that fails, then you'll petition for a sale of the property and a partition of the proceeds."

"Oh, wait, hold on Ron, I think that's a little extreme. We don't have to go that far to settle this thing."

"Well, you tell me. What can you do to settle it?"

"Well, I'm not sure. Sonny won't return my phone calls."

"Tell you what Vasile, you get Sonny to sign the distribution agreement any which way you can. Do whatever you think is appropriate. Don't tell me about it; I don't care how you do it; just do it."

"Okay, Okay. I'll get him in here."

Not that I don't trust Vasile, but I wanted to be sure that the Tax Collector knew what the story was and that whatever back taxes Sonny might owe were his sole obligation. Roberta and I paid a visit to the Town Tax Collector. They were very pleasant. We were directed to the appropriate person, who was also very nice, and assured us that she understood what was going on and would have it straightened out in two shakes of a lamb's tail. But we know better than that, don't we? That lamb's tail would've worn away to the nub.

It took two letters and three telephone calls and another visit to the Tax Collector to get the situation squared away. Finally, it was squared away to our satisfaction; the town put a lien on Sonny's portion of the property (even though he didn't own it yet). A month or so passed. Sister hatchet-face called and asked that we come to the office again. She said that Sonny had come in (Vasile had somehow connived him into doing that under the guise of having some work for him to do, she implied) and signed the document. We did as asked and the distribution agreement was signed. Vasile promised to get it to the probate court and finalize the transaction.

I mentioned to Vasile that when I matched the description of the division in the document to the plot map, it appeared that Roberta would be receiving a few acres more than the formula produced. He replied, "He can read, can't he? If you saw, he saw, or should have seen, it too. If he didn't, that's his problem. I don't think you're under any obligation to bring it to his attention." I asked whether he felt any obligation to point it out. His response was, "I'm not his lawyer. I represent the estate. It doesn't matter to the estate whether he gets a good deal or a bad deal."

Don't you think it's wonderful how lawyers can slip and slide, thieve and hide, all in relation to which way the money is flowing? It's a real talent. One which takes many years of education and a devotion to the art of "distinguishing;" i.e., slicing up the facts, sometimes into microscopic pieces, and then reassembling them (ignoring those unpleasant or nettlesome facts which would impede the march to the conclusion) in such a way that the desired conclusion is at least arguable without getting a red face. That's what we get paid to do. And there are many people who are willing to pay healthy sums to have us do it for them. God I love the law.

We heard nothing for about four months. Then I got another call from hatchet-face. Vasile wants us to visit him; we've got a few things to discuss and he doesn't want to do it on the phone. So we meander to the office. I prophecy to Roberta that the reason he wants us there is that there is a need for more money, he knows he can't get it from Sonny and he's going to whine and snivel about how he can't get the thing done without relying on us to pay whatever needs to be paid. She concedes that my prophecy has a very high likelihood of accuracy. We weren't surprised.

It seems, says Vasile, that in filing the final form to close the estate, there are a number of expenses that we must certify have been paid. The probate judge won't issue a final decree until the form is signed, certified and filed; ergo, we need more money. "Vasile," I say,

"Roberta and I are tired of paying other people's bills, particularly her brother's. The fact of the matter is that we started out in the same place that Sonny did, with the same disadvantages and with the same opportunities. He chose to live his life his way; we chose to better ourselves and by dint of extreme effort, planning and determination have reached a point in our lives where we are comfortable and can afford to pay these expenses, while he cannot afford to subscribe to a newspaper. We are not his keeper. We resent, as a matter of principle, that we are expected to once again "fix" something because we are the only responsible people available. We are inclined to say forget it and demand a sale and partition.

However, out of a sense (perhaps misplaced and undeserved) of familial obligation we are prepared to pay the expenses, on one condition. That condition is that Sonny take on some responsibility by executing a note and mortgage to me for one half of the remaining expenses. We view this as a symbolic condition; but symbols are important in this situation. We want him to recognize that he is a debtor. We don't expect to be repaid. We want to be protected in the event that he is forced to sell some or all of the property.

Once again, I don't care how you do it; but it is your job to get him to sign the note and mortgage.

Failing that, we go back to square one."

Vasile looks concerned. His sister looks concerned. I am concerned. I don't want this damn thing to drag on any more. But Roberta and I want some sort of token, no matter how trifling, that announces that the gravy train has stopped. It is necessary. Vasile says he understands and that he'll have a talk with Sonny. I wish him good luck.

Three weeks later, Vasile calls. He is almost gleeful; he's chatty and obviously pleased with himself.

"Sonny came in this morning. His appointment wasn't until 10:30, but there he was at 10:15. He signed the note and the mortgage and I'll have them on the land records first thing Monday morning. Ha, ha, ha, (cough), ha."

"Well, congratulations, Vasile, how did you manage that?"

"Ha, ha, (cough); well he won't return my calls, so I went up there. Sherry wouldn't let me in the house, but I told her that it was really important that Sonny come to my office because if we couldn't get this squared away, the probate court would issue a summons and the state police would have to come up there to deliver it. Ha, ha, har. You should've seen the look on her face. They don't want any part of the police, ya know? Ya know, there's an outstanding warrant for his arrest on a DWI. Well, ha ha ha, the look on her face! She musta lit a fire under that guy. Anyway, it worked. So I'll get the papers in and we'll get the final order from probate. Okay?"

Well okay.

It was nearly over. True to his word, Vasile filed the note and mortgage deed.

We let him wait about a week, then sent the check that would close the estate. It was a little thing; a little wait for them; I hope a little annoying for them; it was symbolic. The probate court issued its decree. Roberta now owns about 64 acres; 20 of them on a scenic New England pond; she owns a gravel bank; has about 2100 feet of frontage; owns her brother's well - which happens to be on her side of the new property line; and I have a mortgage on Sonny's house and land. The final order of the court, all official looking, signed by the judge, certified as a true and complete copy by the court clerk, and blessed by the official seal of the court, arrived in the mail. It was anti-climactic, just some pieces of paper.

After more than three years from the day we planted Old John, he was finally buried. I hope.

I haven't related all the facts associated with the story. But I think I've given you enough to get a feel for it. It seems that no matter what the facts are, there is always a feel to events that somehow transforms them from mere fact to matters of consequence. Sometimes the consequences, in terms of what meaning and significance we subjectively attach to them, transcend the events themselves and set us on a path we might not have noticed but for the meaning we attribute to them.

Having told you this story, the meaning I attribute to it is that I can't help Sonny (or anyone else) by trying to help him. He's on his own, just like I am; just like we all are. I don't care one wit for the land; that was never a vital factor (Old John could have left it to the boy scouts and I would not have been surprised or disappointed). The important thing about the story is the experience; even if its only use is a kind of perverse pleasure I've taken from telling it to you.

Please give my love to Aunt Virginia. You know that you always have my love and respect (don't push it).

Dot's Rules

Dear Uncle Fred,

I hope that this finds you in reasonably good health. I also hope that you are in the mood for some diversionary light reading.

It is difficult to find the words to tell you the pleasure it gave me to see you again and, particularly, to talk with someone who understands me at an instinctive level. You are virtually the only person I know with whom I can be foul, cynical and sarcastic, and have complete confidence that I will be accepted as I am. I really appreciate it.

As you know, I have spent the better part of the last 14 months in Florida, tending to the needs, wants, desires and demands of my mother-in-law, Dot. The only reason I have subjected myself to her unpleasant presence is that I am in love with her daughter (my current spouse - Roberta[13]). I also had some affection for Dot's husband, Bob, a man I've spoken of briefly in prior letters. I haven't told you much about Dot, but that doesn't mean that there is nothing to tell; quite the contrary. Stories about Dot could fill a small book. I'm not going to impose on you with a full-blown exposition, but I think I can give you some "flavor" of what she is like in a relatively few pages.

---

[13] Of course, Roberta is the only spouse I've ever had. It's a joke for Pete's sake.

I think you would agree that it is in the nature of human beings to try to impose some sort of order on nature and events. It can't be done, of course, because nature and events will do whatever they do whether we want it that way or not. Most of us, therefore, adopt a certain construct which we use to anticipate (or predict) the future, knowing that whatever we predict or whatever we plan will be subject to revision or abandonment depending on whatever facts and circumstances are, in fact, extant in the future; facts and circumstances which are currently unknown and largely unknowable. As the V - man says: "Everything in life is adjustable; life itself is adjustable."

There are some people, however, who are intellectually or emotionally unable to comprehend the reality that reality is randomly variable; that the order we perceive in nature and human affairs is a veneer, a mask, largely of our own hopeful creation and which screens us from the underlying, almost wholly unpredictable, chaos. My mother-in-law is one of those people.

It isn't easy to describe Dot. She's one of those things you just can't appreciate unless you see and hear it in operation. She was born some 67 years ago to Bill and Florence. Bill was a Navy man, ne'er do well, and heavy drinker who was forced to exit Dot's life by Florence when she divorced him.

Any relationship between Dot and Bill thereafter was prevented by Bill's premature demise (cause listed as TB-alcoholism). According to Dot, however, her mother was the cause of Bill's death. In this version of reality Florence had somehow driven Bill crazy and to extinction, and the proof is that he died in a sanitarium. The more credible version of reality is that Bill's behavior drove Florence to seek the extraordinary remedy, for that era, of divorce. He then drank himself into an immunosuppressive chronic stupor that permitted the TB to gain an advantage that (in the absence of effective treatments) could not be overcome and led to his death in a *sanatorium*.

This latter version is supported by the testimony of reliable witnesses and documents related to the divorce proceedings and medical records.

The facts notwithstanding, Dot remains adamant, "That old bitch killed my fathuh!" Incidentally, the credible evidence would disclose to a reasonable person that Wild Bill (as he was called) was a negative factor in the community and there wasn't a wet eye anywhere when word of his passing got around.

Still, the effect was that Dot had no permanent adult male person present during her early life. What she did have was her mother, her mother's sister Aunt Lucy (a spinster) and Nana (mother of Florence, Lucy, et al) an aged widow. By Dot's account, growing up in the household of the Wallen women was akin to being raised by Shakespeare's three weird sisters of toil and trouble fame. I have no way of assaying this assertion because Nana was not around by the time I met Roberta, and Florence and Lucy were well into an enfeebled and harmless dotage. Whatever family nastiness the sisters may have been able to recall was never discussed in my presence.

I do know that the sisters had three brothers: Clarence, Arthur and Ernest. The last of these was still with us when I became enamored of Roberta (about 35 years ago). I had the opportunity to speak with him on several occasions. He was a regular sort of guy who worked, married, and had a family, all in the normal course. The other two are shadow figures, moving in and out of the weird sisters' household on an irregular basis depending on the state of their finances and their need for sustenance. Neither produced progeny, which is as it should be, I suspect.

Aunt Lucy owned the house the family lived in. The only permanent inhabitants for many years were Florence and Dot; Aunt Lucy worked in Boston and stayed on the homestead weekends and holidays. The home was, however, temporary quarters for Arthur, Clarence and sundry other persons, most related, but some not. The only constant in the ebb and flow of activity was the guiding hands of Florence and Aunt Lucy. But this matriarchy had some drawbacks; namely, Dot had no balance, no opposing view; no yang for the constant yin, no model of loutish, slovenly, straight line thinking, worry-about-it-if-it-happens, maleness. This was a defect in her environment.

Unfortunately, it was not the only defect to which she was subject. Nature was not kind to her in the arrangement of the gray matter it had dispensed. Dot was not an academically inclined child. Whatever there was to work with was not developed to any significant degree by the educational system. Dot left school after the sixth grade. Why would anyone, especially a girl, want to or need to finish school?

So what we have today (and have had for the 35 or so years that I've know her) is a woman who looks like an adult, but who, in fact, attained the intellectual and emotional level of a 14 year old and stopped growing. Like any other 14 year old, she is not equipped to manage the vagaries of the world through contemplation. With no grounding in a perspective that permits toleration of the infinite variability of reality within a construct that takes account of and accommodates unpredictability, Dot is bound in what psychologists call the "concrete" stage. She sees the world in terms of "rules."

The lynch pin of order is a schedule. Eating is the obvious schedule that accords with the most fundamental of human needs. Using food as a lynch pin is not only natural, it satisfyingly splits the 24 hour period of the day into measurable segments of clearly defined and manageable duration. With the morning comes the start of the active portion of the day, and this segment is marked by breakfast. Immediately upon rising, the coffee pot is plugged in. That is all that is necessary because the contents are prepared the prior evening, just before retiring (no later than 9 P.M.). It is then necessary to go to the bathroom, followed by taking the dog for a walk. Upon the completion of those tasks, coffee is poured and cereal placed in a bowl of whole milk (the reason for the adjective will be explained), to be taken onto the porch and there consumed. Each activity is taken in precisely the same sequence regardless of month, season or weather.

Some restrictions apply. Having had the daily ration of coffee, no additional cups of joe may be consumed until 24 hours have elapsed. The existence of this last rule had escaped me until an unpleasant dining experience with Dot and Roberta at the Cracker Barrel restaurant. In an effort, I think, to make conversation Roberta said,

"Gee, Ma, I notice that you only drink coffee in the morning and never during the rest of the day." [A tautology , but we find it helpful to double-up our statements to Dot so that if she misses one part she might be able to ascertain the import of the first from the alternate statement]

"Roberta! Ya don't drink coffee aftuh breakfass!"

"Why not? If you drink it in the morning, then why not later in the day?"

"Becuz my mothuh didn't let me have it latuh. That's why!"

"Yeah [in the tone of a question and a conjunction] but Big Nana's been dead for 15 years and you're 67 years old."

"Roberta, it isn't allowed! And I don't wanna hear 'coffee' any mowah! It pisses me off when people talk about it!"

I guess that settles that. I have dutifully removed the word "coffee" from my lexicon (whatever a lexicon is).

Many of the rules pertain to the acquisition, preparation, allocation and consumption of food. For example:

a) Roberta's family, as you may recall, ran a dairy farm for a number of generations. The herd consisted, at various times, of 60 to 90 registered Jersies. When I went off to law school, the family's interest in the farm was waning (I certainly wanted nothing to do with it), with the result that no one really wanted to continue its operation or management. Since Clara (Roberta's grandmother) was too old to run the place, she decided to sell the herd. This she did. The cows were sold, packed on a cattle truck, and hauled the 1300 miles to their new home at the T.G. Lee farm in Florida.

Of course, Dot had always had milk produced by the herd while she (and it) lived in R.I. When she (and Bob) moved to Florida, it was only natural that the tradition be kept intact. The only brand of milk she will buy is T.G. Lee. I don't have a problem with that. I do have a problem, however, with the milk rule: "no one in the family can buy anythin' but T.G. Lee, and if they do, then goddammit, I won't drink it, or eat anythin' made with it, and that's that!"

b) Scheduling of meals is one of the first of the daily tasks. Whenever we are in Florida, the first incoming telephone call of the morning is from Dot, and the first topic of discussion is when and where the noon meal is to be had. The noon meal means the noon meal. Lunch cannot be had any later than 12:30, post-meridian. If, perchance, lunch has not been consumed by that time, then her "belly thinks my throat's been cut" and she is "ovuh the hump" and will "probably nevuh eat again." Thus, it is imperative that plans be made no later than 9:45 A.M. and schedules coordinated to effectuate the imperative.

c) The food to be eaten, if it is to be prepared and eaten in someone's home (hers or ours), must include bread, lots of salt and pepper, real butter, and the ever present T.G. Lee (coffee being not an option). Consumption at her home can be dangerous to one's health. One must never agree to bacon and eggs for lunch. Not that I have anything against bacon and eggs, but the method of preparation is this: first fry the bacon, remove when thoroughly fried, place eggs (which must be brown eggs) in bacon fat, fry eggs; place slimy eggs next to slimy bacon on plate; place toasted bread saturated with real butter on plate, consume contents of plate and wash down with whole milk from T.G. Lee. We call this arteriosclerosis *a la* Dot.

d) It is virtually impossible to find fish or fruit in Dot's house. Bob didn't like fruit so it wasn't, and isn't, purchased. Fish "ain't meat" so that isn't purchased either. Meals are, therefore, of the meat and potato genre. The potatoes are always heavily laden with real butter, plenty of pepper and huge quantities of salt. The potatoes are mashed, then those ingredients are joined by whole milk from T.G. Lee. The meat always has a gravy "tah go with it" which is made from whatever liquefied fats ("the drippins") the meat exuded during cooking.

71

e) Food preparation has its own set of rules. Rule number one is that any utensil used, must be used only once, for a specific purpose, and not used again. For example, the pot used to boil potatoes is used only for that purpose. That pot cannot be used to serve the potatoes; rather another utensil - a bowl - must be used for serving. A spoon, knife or fork used in preparation of food must not be used for consumption of food. Each food item must be served in its separate container (not the same as the one used for any previous operation) and must have its own (and appropriate) serving utensil, which must be placed in the utensil containing the food item.

A spoon, for example, used (or to be used) to apportion a particular food item, cannot be used to apportion any other food item. The result of this task-specific utilization is that the preparation and consumption of even the simplest meal produces a mound of dirty "dishes," and a major operation (like a Thanksgiving meal) requires every pot, pan, dish, bowl, fork, spoon and knife in the house. While she would be flabbergasted and angry at the suggestion, in effect Dot keeps a kosher kitchen.

f) Each food preparation operation must be accomplished according to a strict formula. For example:

"Roberta! What ah you doin!"
"What does it look like I'm doing? I'm cutting a tomato."
"Not like that! You don't cut it that way, you have tuh cut it the othuh way!"
"Why?"
"Because that's the way you have tuh do it! Don't you know anything?" [The "g" ordinarily omitted, is added where emphasis is desired.]
"I know I can cut a tomato anyway I want."
"No you can't! I guess I just didn't have you long enough tuh teach you the right way tuh do things. [This is a reference to the fact that Roberta was the responsibility of Florence and Aunt Lucy for the first five years of her life, and was out of Dot's house by the time she was 16.] "You can't even peel an orange the right way."
"What is the right way, Ma?"
"The way I do it. Hmpf"
Well, case closed. That Roberta didn't learn the right way to do things was, on another occasion, abundantly demonstrated by her dishwashing technique. I was sitting on the porch after a noon meal, when Dot appeared at the door with her hands on her hips and a smile on her face.
"Ronnie, come see what yaw wife is doin'."
"I can see what she's doing [through the kitchen window]. She's washing dishes."

"Yeah, but come see. [I get up and come see.] Look."

"Look at what?"

"Doncha see? She's puttin' the spoons in the rack upside down." [Sure enough, spoons - and other implements - were this way and that, higgledy piggledy, in the drying rack.]

"Which way is upside down?"

"The othuh way!"

"Which way?"

"The othuh way, I tol' ya!!"

"But which way is the other way?"

"Oh, for chrize sake, the othuh way. Yaw as dumb as yowuh wife!"

g) Food schedule rules also apply to non-human entities. Dot has had any number of animals over the years, including a raccoon, a monkey, a parrot and an alligator. But for the most part she has had dogs. Her favorite type of dog - and thus the type that she has had more of than any other - is a pug. I don't know how much you know about dogs. A pug has, as its name implies, a pushed in ("pug") face. It is about the size of a cat, short-haired, with short, Floppy little ears, spindly little legs supporting a chunky body, and a curled, pig - like, tail. Because of its "pug" face, it is incapable of producing a meaningful bark; it cannot use its jaws to inflict a serious bite; and it constantly wheezes, snorts and slimes. In other words, it is a grotesque parody of a dog and, not insignificantly, resembles Dot.

The latest version of this type of dog is called Candy. Candy must eat, of course. Therefore, a schedule of feeding is required.

"Ronnie, we hafta get home."

"Why?"

"I hafta feed Candy."

"Okay. When I finish my coffee, we'll go." [I have declined to follow the coffee rule.]

"But it's quatuh tuh six!"

"So?"

"It's almost six!"

"You've told me what time it is twice now. What does it mean?"

"I tol' you! Candy has tuh eat!"

"What's that got to do with what time it is?"

"She has tuh eat at six!"

"Ma, a dog doesn't know what time it is."

"Yes she does, she knows!"

"How does she handle daylight saving time?"

"Oh, you piss me off!"

Perhaps the most disturbing and disconcerting Dot characteristic has nothing to do with an explicit rule; rather it has to do with an assumption or, more accurately, a presumption, which it has proved impossible to rebut. Specifically, the presumption is that Roberta and I, and anyone else within earshot, know what she is talking about. I'll relate a classic example, but first a little explanation.

You will recall that my brother-in-law, Sonny, is (among other things) a highly skilled mason. Over the years the stress of lifting and moving heavy objects (like rocks) has produced over-extension of portions of the intestinal wall, resulting in two hernias. This condition is, I'm told, quite uncomfortable. I'm also told that it is inadvisable to allow the condition to continue without correction. Nevertheless, Sonny's condition has existed for many years. He declines to seek medical treatment, partly because he has no insurance, and partly because of his distrust and fear of doctors. I cannot fault him for his distrust of the practitioners of the alleged healing arts. My experience with this putatively learned group is almost wholly negative. I think you have had enough experience of your own to understand when I say that I will, full of trepidation, seek their aid only in the event of extreme, unremitting pain or imminent demise.

Sonny's condition is a topic of conversation between and among his mother, his sister and his significant other (Sherry). To her credit, Roberta does not initiate such discussions, but during her infrequent telephone talks with Sherry and her weekly talk with Mommy-Dearest, the subject is mentioned. But they don't discuss the subject to any meaningful extent with Sonny. It occurs to me that women oftentimes talk a topic to death with anyone other than the person central to the issue. Why is that? My father taught me, and I have taught my sons, that if you have anything to say about another person (particularly another man) you say it directly to his face.

Anyway, Roberta was talking with Dot, and the conversation went something like this:

"So I was talkin' with Sherry an' ... poor Sonny ... she said his onions ah gettin' so-o-o big."

"Why 'poor' Sonny?"

"Becuz his onions ah so big!"

"What's wrong with that? Doesn't he want big onions? He could just pick them before they get big, couldn't he?"

"Oh, fuh chrise sake, Berta, his onions … his onions!!"

"Ma, what the hell are you talking about?"

"Oh, jessuz, don't you know nothin'? The onions between his legs! Jessuz, you ah so dumb."

"I'm dumb? Why don't you use the right word?"

"That's what Sherry calls 'em. Whadda you call 'em?"

"How about their anatomically correct name: testicles?"

"Testicles? Who ever says that? Chrise, I didn't heyuh the word 'penis' 'til I was twelve years old."

"What did you call it?"

"I call it its ... ana-atomic ... correct name: cock! Hee-heee."

"You're all class, Ma."

"Yeah, that's right. So, I tol' Sherry ta tell Sonny ta come down heyuh an' have it done, an' I'll pay for it."

"Why down there? Why not just send him the money - or better - send the money to the doctor?"

"'Cause, if I'm payin' it's gonna be done by Doctuh Rod. [Dr. Rodman - the guy who was supposedly going to take the foot out of Dot's colon] Doctuh Rod says if his hernia breaks he'll bleed ta death."

"I don't know about that, I think general peritonitis would kill him."

"Gen'ral who? Whaddaya talkin' about? Who's that?"

"Never mind."

Now, you know as well as I that in the vast majority of our normal, everyday, common conversations, a great deal of information is not expressed. We rely on each other to gather the unexpressed information from general knowledge, from an appreciation of the text, context and intertext, from shared information about family, friends and associates; from reasonably apparent inferences derived from the specific context in which the explicit statements are made; from prior explicit statements and natural inferences therefrom; from the general tone, import, and apparent objective of the text; and from the emphasis, pauses and gesticulations of the speaker.[14] Most of us, even when we are face to face with our audience, understand that that audience needs a certain amount of basic information of the explicit kind; some indication of context; some identified referents; some sort of verbal cues (or clues) which the hearer can use as a basis to perform the task of filling the gaps we leave in the narrative.[15] Not Dot.

Dot's deficiency in this regard begins at a fundamental, grammatical level. For example, it appears that she cannot conjugate verbs:

"The othuh day I wuz theyuh, and he come down. Then Pat, she come down. Next thing, I see him, an' an' ... ya know, he come right ovuh tuh me like nothin' happened."

It would be one thing, and an annoying thing, if verb conjugation were the only failing, but as the little example shows, it is not the only failing. First, this declaration was delivered without any sort of introduction. Time, place, persons and circumstances were undefined. Not only did I not know

---

[14] I expect that you will have something to say about this overly long sentence. Feel free.

[15] Ditto

who the first "he" was, or where he had come from or to, I didn't know who the "him" referred to in "he come right ovuh" was or whether he was the same as "he," and if he wasn't, where "him" came from. Moreover, I haven't the foggiest why it was a surprise [which I, perhaps erroneously, inferred] that he "come right 'ovuh," nor did I have any notion of what might have happened to explain the "like nothin' happened" clause. Now, you're probably thinking, "Well, she isn't all bad, she did say "Pat." Yes, she did, but to my knowledge, there are three (female) Pats that "Pat" could have been. Unwilling to engage Dot in an analysis of the statement, or prompt further ambiguous statements by way of attempted explanation on her part, I said,

"Uh huh."

While most of the persons we know in common with Dot have expressed the same reaction to Dot's disjointed, ambiguous, and confusing mode of discourse, we ride with it by saying "uh huh," smiling and nodding; or just waiting until she stops. The only time an explanation is asked for is if a question mark can be inferred from the statement, and it seems that some response is necessary, or where curiosity gets the better of us and we ask for more information.

"Jim, he was married tuh, ya know ... ah, whatsername. You know, her mothuh was the Clemens girl? Maybe ya don't. I went tuh school with her. Her fathuh ran the grocery store before the flood in '54. Anyway, they moved tuh ... ah ... someplace out theyuh. Dad was drivin' then, and this was aftuh he was gone ...Dad went ovuh tuh see her when he was out theyuh, an' she made a mistake. ..."

"What was it?"

"What?"

"You said she made a mistake."

"Yeah, she did, that's all."

"Well, what was it?"

"I tol' ya, he wuz ovuh theyuh and she made a mistake!"

"Wait ... wait ... I got it! ... She cooked Dad a steak?"

"That's what I've been sayin' for chrizze sake. Doncha unerstan' English for chrizze sake? Jezzuz chrise almighty, you make me crazy!"

"I guess I didn't understand what you were saying."

"Well, if ya'd jus' goddam listen once in a while, maybe I wouldn't hafta repeat everythin'."

That might be true. But there is a certain amount of, not easily tolerated, stress associated with listening to her.

During our last stay in Florida, Roberta was having difficulty with a sinus infection. This led her to seek professional assistance from an alleged medical doctor with whom her parents had had some dealings in the recent past: one Mahumat Sharkit. Like 90% of the medical doctors affiliated with the local hospital Sharkit is an immigrant. I don't know his place of birth, but suspect it is Iran or Pakistan. It is almost impossible to find any medical type at the hospital whose first language is English. Why this country of some 200+ millions in population cannot find within its native ranks enough people capable of graduating medical school is quite beyond me. Am I the only one who has noticed the dearth of English speaking doctors? Why do my tax and social security "contribution" dollars go to support immigrants in a life style that compares favorably with a foreign potentate; a lifestyle superior to the vast majority of people born in this country? (Why am I asking you?)

In any event, Roberta made an appointment with Mahumat. When Roberta goes to the doctor in Connecticut she goes alone. But, apparently, when one visits a doctor in Florida, one cannot go alone. Dot must go also. This is curious, since Dot has never paid motherly attention to her children (Roberta and Sonny of the "I shot the bird" incident). Dot lives in an egocentric universe. No event, circumstance, or other fact or consequence has any meaning to Dot except as it relates to her. She asks but one question of the world: "what about me?" So I was somewhat surprised when Roberta told me that her mother wanted to go to the doctor's office with her.

Through circumstances not within my conscious recollection, I was dragooned into going as well. I think that the rationale for my inclusion ran like this: Dot had to go with Roberta; Dot couldn't stand to travel in my car because the back seat is too low; thus, the use of her Lincoln Town Car was necessary, and because the office is about 10 miles away she couldn't possibly drive all that way, so I would have to drive. You'll notice that this sorites is incomplete.[16] It doesn't account for the fact that Roberta (who is an excellent driver and has driven buses and tractor trailers) could just as easily have driven the Lincoln. Be that as it may, I was assigned to drive.

On the drive:

"Berta, do you want me tuh come in with ya?"

"No."

"Why not?"

"Why?"

"I always went in with Dad."

"I'm not Dad."

"But I always go in."

"Not with me."

A short while later:

"Ah ya shoowuh ya don't want me tuh come in with ya?"

"I'm sure."

"Why not?"

"Because I'm a big girl. I can handle this myself."

"But I always went with Dad so I could talk tuh the doctuh."

---

[16] "Sorites" is a fancy word for a series of statements (premises) followed by a conclusion. I used it in an attempt to goad Uncle Fred into making some sort of nasty comment. He didn't.

"I can do my own talking."

"Huhrmph! I did the talkin' for Dad."

"That was part of the problem."

"I did everythin' for that man."

"Like I said ..."

At the office Roberta headed to the door with Dot, looking dejected, trailing her. The good doctor wasn't there. He was still at the hospital, no doubt performing some lifesaving function (i.e., unnecessary or useless tests ordered for the dual purpose of providing a defense in the event of malpractice litigation and paying for the expensive equipment used in the test) for which he would receive outrageous sums of money from the federal and state governments, one or more insurance companies and the patient (i.e., victim). After a while, Mahumat showed up, driving what appeared to be a spanking new luxury class car made in Japan. How fitting.

"Berta, can't I come in with yuh?"

"No."

"Yowuh bein' mean."

"Look, Ma, if you want this appointment, take it. If not, go wait in the car with Ron. I am quite capable of doing this all by myself. I've done it for decades and I don't need or want you with me."

Unfortunately for me, Dot did as she was told.

"Little Miss Independent won't let me go in with her."

"Why should she?"

"I always went in with Dad."

"Like she said, she isn't Dad. If I don't go with her to the doctor, why should you? When I go to the doctor [I have no doctor and if there is a god I won't ever see one] she doesn't go with me. Did you ever hear of the doctor-patient privilege? Don't you think your presence would inhibit a free flow of information between the doctor and his patient? Isn't your presence irrelevant and intrusive?"

"Huh?"

"Which word didn't you understand?"

[softly] "Most of 'em."

"Never mind, then."

For the next hour and a half Dot regaled me with a series of depressing, self-pitying, vignettes of her life experiences, delivered in a chronologically confused, halting, monosyllabic narrative, all of which related to some event (most from her childhood) which she perceived as demonstrating how abused and misunderstood she had been, and why she was now so deserving of sympathy. It was a wholly unpleasant performance that, instead of eliciting any feeling of empathy, produced its opposite.

It is a tribute to my patience, my intellectual discipline, my experience with the consequences of violent behavior (but mostly my fear of Roberta's reaction), that I suppressed the desire to shove an ice pick in her ear. The thought of doing that was comforting and is a device I have used to keep the promise I make to myself every day that I will not kill anything, today. Normally, it's easy to maintain control by simply picturing the object of my disgust with a fragmentation grenade taped in his (or her) mouth with my finger looped in the pin. I know you prefer phosphorous and I respect that; to each his own. But, I digress.

After an ungodly long time, Dot seemed to run out of energy, or interest, I don't know which. Perhaps the total absence of any response to her tales of woe didn't give her the reinforcement she needed or wanted. Whatever; she stopped talking, got out of the car and went into the office. Roberta was in the process of leaving, having spent all of 10 minutes (or, in monetary terms, $125, American) with Mahumat. She was discussing, with the alleged nurse, some point related to a prescription when Dot approached and said:

"Whuddy say about me?"

Enough said? I think so.

Perhaps I've missed the point of this. Perhaps the cosmic consciousness has visited this baleful baggage on me in order to teach me (or I might learn) something of pity. Perhaps I am to take away from the Dot experience some profound, ineffable, transcendent message, an epiphany. If I could just use the experience to break through into the underlying unity of all existence, the sameness, the one-ness of us all, perhaps I could attain enlightenment.

Yeah, ... and perhaps if dogs had square assholes they'd shit bricks.

I'll leave you alone now. Our love to you and Aunt Virginia.

How To

Dear Uncle Fred,

I believe enough time has elapsed since I last inflicted upon you the tiresome task of reading one of my interminably tedious letters to do it again. The last time I wrote, I told you a little about my dysfunctional mother-in-law. As you know, Roberta [and/or one or more of my children - usually Darlene, Rhonda or John] reads everything I write. This is not as much fun as you might think, because as part of the task Roberta also reads my business communications and currently is plodding through the book I told you I was writing (legal methodology -a/k/a "a miracle cure for insomnia"). When my children read the letter about Dot's Rules, they thought it captured the essence of Dot and that it was, in the main, humorous. When Roberta read it, the reaction was a bit different.

As always, it is my intention and hope that in forcing these stories on you, you will be amused or at least entertained for a while. Toward that end I sometimes use a degree of emphasis that may attribute more significance to certain aspects of the story than they, in Roberta's opinion, warrant. She says that I exaggerate. While there is some truth in that assertion, it is also true that I have not manufactured from whole cloth any of the incidents I have related to you.

They are as near to the factual circumstances as my less than total recall can retrieve. She did not accuse me of any exaggeration in connection with the Dot's Rules letter. Her reaction was that it was not funny. I think she's been too close to the situation to appreciate its comic elements. She also noted that some of my letters have depicted some of her kin in a less than complimentary light. She is not saying that they deserve a glowing report, but that I have not depicted any members of my own family with similar strokes.

My defense to this charge is that you know more about the eccentricity, outright insanity and dirty laundry in my family than I do, and it would be pointless to tell you stories that you already know. I think that is an accurate assessment. You may disagree. If that's the case, let me know and I'll do the best I can to provide my version of those matters with respect to which you may have incomplete or non-credible information. [chripes, that's an awful sentence; but I'm too lazy to fix it]. Unless you advise me to the contrary, I will continue to tell you about the more interesting characters that we've encountered (some of whom are her relatives) and will continue to describe persons and events from my own, admittedly subjective and perverse, perspective.

You may find this attitude a bit presumptuous, but it should not surprise you. As you may have observed, been told, or discerned, I was not an easy child. I was a less easy adolescent, and a decidedly difficult young man. I don't know with any certainty where this attitude came from initially, or why it evolved with such vigor. I have decided that it is not a paternal trait. Certainly, the V - man is not responsible (although the only DiBiassi I knew - my grandmother - was not marked by a passive personality). Neither the Me nor the Funge seem to be tainted with this personality flaw; it seems to me that they are like my father's side both physically and mentally. I, on the other hand, am distinguishable from my father and brothers physically and, more significantly, by an irascible nature (thus the sobriquet - "the other one"). No, I think the finger of accusation must be pointed at the maternal (your) side.

I don't want to engage you in a debate. I could be persuaded that my analysis is in error if you could provide solid, corroborated, evidence in opposition; but at this point I think it is enough to say that if I am not a nice guy it is largely due to your side of the family. Don't misunderstand. I'm not saying that you're all infected with the bad gene, but some were and are. For example, Uncle Godfrey isn't, but you and I are. Also, I'm not saying that we are uniformly unpleasant; and I'm not saying that most of our unpleasantness isn't justified. I am saying that we are predisposed to react in sometimes unpredictable and socially unacceptable ways when confronted with situations not to our liking (which, unfortunately and through no fault of our own, occur almost daily).

I make these comments only because they occurred to me as a result of Roberta's reaction to my last letter. They are, I think, irrelevant to the little stories that follow.

It may be difficult to imagine, but I was once a young lawyer. My law school education was not exactly an intellectually satisfying experience, although it was certainly an education. The method of teaching was the Socratic method. This meant that the professor assigned a preposterous number of cases to be read; expected that each student would read and retain every word of each case; and be prepared to respond immediately and appropriately to any question he might ask about the facts of the case, its procedural history, the issues and the principles involved, the method of analysis, the arguments of counsel and the bearing and value of any cases cited in the court's opinion.

In practice, the professor would pick some unfortunate student and ask a series of questions that would eventually stupefy the poor victim until he could no longer respond to any additional inquiry. The express object of this sadistic exercise was to "prepare " the student to "think on his feet." The unexpressed object was, in many cases, to make the professor feel good. Some of the professors had never practiced, and would never practice, law in their lives. It was normally these academicians who enjoyed the method.

I did learn a lot about the law in law school; enough to pass the bar exam; but not enough to be a lawyer.

My first legal job was with a small law firm (disbanded more than 20 years ago) As the "kid" in the firm, I was given (I didn't bring in any clients) those cases where there was no real danger of harm to the firm if I screwed up; e.g., slip and falls, minor auto accidents, divorce and landlord-tenant disputes. My first court appearance took place when the boss (call him Mr. Calamari) said:

"Go over to GA 19 and when they call Dilwitty v. Henn, say over."

"Huh?"

"Just say over."

"What does it mean?"

"Just do it. I don't have time to explain everything."

"But don't I need to know what it's about? The facts? The file?"

"Ya don't need anything, kid. Just say over."

So I went off to court prepared to say "over" but without a clue if anyone asked me anything. I arrived in the courtroom in time to hear this exchange between the judge and a young lawyer.

"... but your honor, this was an odd hoke committee, granted authority only to ...."

"A moment, counselor. What did you say?"

"I said the odd hoke committee was granted ..."

"Stop! Stop! ODD HOKE? What is the meaning of that? What are you trying to say?"

"With respect, your honor, the committee was granted very limited authority for a specific purpose and ...."

"So you want the court to understand that it was an ad hoc committee?"

"How's that?"

"AD HOC"

"Well, ... yes ... if that's the way you want to say it."

"It is. Continue."

"Well, since its authority was limited, its action in this matter was ooltrah wireeys."

"It was WHAT?"

"Ooltrah wireeys, your honor."

"My god! Are you trying to say *ultra vires*, my boy?"

"I don't know that phrase, your honor."

"Are you a member of the bar?"

"Why. . . yes. . . of course. . . sir. . ."

"Then you went to college and law school and passed the bar exam, yes?"

"Yes, your honor."

"I did too, my lad. How does it come that we are not speaking the same language?"

"But, your honor, it is the language I was taught."

"Taught? Taught? You may have been taught to butcher the language passed on to us by a hundred generations of judges, but I was not. I was taught to respect the traditional pronunciation as I was taught to respect the tradition of law itself. It is not the province of the discredited educational system of this country [even then academia was viewed with disdain] to pervert or malign a single jot or tittle in the law or its language. It may be fashionable among the parasitic members of society to question and demand change in any tradition the productive members of our society hold dear [you'll recall that "hippies" were in vogue], but I for one will turn a blind eye - or shall I say a deaf ear - to these pusillanimous, misguided and silly affronts.

Are we to have the common man change his ways? Should he say STAYTOOUS QWUOWOH when he means status quo; KIRKAY when he means circa; and PERKENTOOUM for percent? I think not. Until someone brings forward a tape recording of Julius Caesar - that's HOOLYOWUS KAYZAR to you, my boy- speaking to his troops, this court will tolerate no Latin pronunciation that departs from tradition. You, lad, and all you other attorneys in this room, mark me well. Any mispronunciation and I will hold you in contempt. I know this may work a hardship on some new members of the bar. That cannot be helped. I will not have pig Latin spoken here.

Clerk, put this case over [over !! ??] and call the calendar." [huh?]

I had, as you know, been educated by Catholic monks. The fathers often spoke Latin conversationally to bar the students from obtaining inside information. Their pronunciation accorded with the "traditional" legal pronunciation, so I had no problem in this context. Now, you may think this little exchange trivial, but I think it was significant. It appeared that not only did the judge have control over what was said, but how it sounded, and could threaten contempt of court for even a minor infraction like pronunciation. Talk about authority.

Incidentally, some of my students have informed me of my mispronunciations. I tell them what the judge said. Anyway, I speak English with an accent, and to my ear so do they. Who is right is a question of who has authority, that's all. Back to the story.

So, I'm sitting there ready to say "over." The judge had instructed the clerk to put the case "over." That caught my attention, but it didn't help me understand the consequences of saying it. The very first case called by the clerk was mine. Shit!

I stood up, said in a clear voice, "over" and sat down. The clerk called another case. Another person stood up, said "over" and left. I sat for a while. Other calls received the same response. The respondents left. I left.

I returned to the office and asked one of the secretaries what I had done [the secretaries knew more than I did at this point]. She said,

"You put the case off for two weeks."

"I did?"

"Yeah. Over means you want it put off for two weeks. They'll call it again in two weeks."

"You mean I don't need an excuse, like I was sick, I had to go to the dentist, my dog ate my brief?"

"No. That's it. Say over and it's postponed for two weeks."

"How many times can I do that?"

[impatiently] "I suppose until the judge gets annoyed."

"So, I could postpone a case indefinitely?"

"I suppose. We do it all the time."

How marvelous. I had the power to delay legal reckoning by the utterance of a single word: I could frustrate my opponent and the entire legal process for weeks, maybe months! They didn't tell me about this in law school. God I love the law.

But I had much more to learn, and A. Frank Calamari was the man to teach me. He was a founding partner, in his late 30s; short, squat and swarthy. He looked like an over-wide fire hydrant with a head on it. His parents had come from Sicily and he spoke a variant of Italian I had never heard before. The syntax seemed to be Italian, but the words sounded foreshortened and phrases were elided into a stream of sound that made their meaning, to me, impenetrable. A. Frank's English was, however, impeccable, as was his Latin. The meaning of the "A." was a closely held secret. I suspect it was something horrendously ethnic, like Annunciato, but I would never know.

One of the first bits of tutoring I received from A. Frank was that in divorce actions where we represented the female spouse, the policy of the firm was to shoot for a "50/50 compromise." Specifically, the goal in such cases was that the wife get the house, the husband get the mortgage; the wife get the car, the husband get the payments; the wife get the kids, the husband pay support; the wife stay at home, the husband pay alimony. With this goal in mind, we could be assured of protracted negotiations with opposing counsel; thus a basketful of billable hours; thus a big fee; paid for, of course, by the husband. This would also have the salutary effect of endearing us to the wife, who would tell all her similarly situated friends of our good work; thus ensuring a continuing string of referrals.

I was also encouraged to make the most of the limited trial experience I would get from my silly little cases. As I said, the cases assigned to me were minor in virtually all respects, except their educational value. For example, each case, no matter how trivial, presented the opportunity to test the particular judge's boundaries of permissiveness, and the acuity of the particular opposing counsel. Let me explain what I mean by an example.

A client had slipped on the stairs of a tenement house as she approached her second floor apartment. She said the stairs were dark and that the steps themselves were loose and in a neglected state. Her injuries were slight, but she was out of pocket a few hundred dollars for medical expenses that her insurance didn't cover. We sued the landlord. He had insurance. Why the attorneys for the insurance company wouldn't settle, I have no idea. What comes to mind is the old story about the one lawyer in town who is living in poverty until another lawyer sets up shop in the same town, and both of them become wealthy. In any event, the insurance company wouldn't settle, so we went to trial.

[After calling the case and ascertaining that counsel were present and prepared to proceed]

[Judge Recht]: "Mr. Villanova, you represent Mrs. Spidorsky?"

"Yes, your honor."

"Will you approach the bench? [What the hell is this about?]. Mr. Villanova, you're with Calamari aren't you?"

"Yes, sir."

"Hasn't he spoken with you about proper court appearance?"

"I don't take your meaning, your honor."

"My meaning, Villanova, is your hair."

"My hair?"

"Yes. Hasn't Frank talked to you about hair?"

"Your honor, Frank has almost no hair, at least not on his head."

"Are you being obtuse, Villanova? Your hair is long."

"But, your honor, with respect, the length of my hair has nothing to do with my ability to represent Mrs. Spidorsky."

"Listen up, kid. It has nothing to do with ability, but it has everything to do with the appearance of ability and, not incidentally, the attitude of this court toward your presentation. Get it cut; off the collar and above the ears."

"Your honor is most persuasive."

With that piece of business out of the way we proceeded. Mrs. Spidorsky was a handsome, older woman who made a good appearance, spoke well and with confidence and clearly had the sympathy of an otherwise bored jury. The facts were simple. It was an unexciting process to bring them out. My opposite number seemed to have little interest in the recitation of facts, and asked only a few questions of Mrs. Spidorsky on cross. He then called his only witness, the building superintendent, who testified, in essence, that he always did a good job of maintaining the place and that Mrs. S. should have been more careful because she knew the stairway light was out. It was a pretty sleepy afternoon, so I decided to take some liberties.

"Mr. Kurtz, you say Mrs. Spidorsky knew the light was out. How do you know that?"

"It was out when she left the building that morning."

"What time was that?"

"About 9."

"When did you notice that the light was out?"

"About 7."

"So you knew the light was out at seven?"

"Yeah. That's what I said."

"So you knew it was out all day. Why didn't you change the bulb?"

"I didn't get to it."

"You allowed that defective condition to exist?" [I expected an objection here, but I heard none. The judge took no notice either. I think he was doing a crossword]

"Yeah."

"Also, Mr. Kurtz, you don't deny that the steps were loose, do you?"

"No."

"And would you say that that made the steps themselves defective?" [Kurtz hesitated. There should have been an objection here, the question called for a conclusion by the witness. The judge did notice this, and looked at defense counsel, who was also doing a crossword, I think. I looked at Recht. He looked at me. We looked at opposing counsel. Recht shrugged and, with his pencil, made a circular motion at Kurtz]

"Yeah, I guess so."

I thought that should do it. The jury didn't leave the box. They awarded Mrs. Spidorsky $2,500, plus attorney fees, not a piddling amount for 1967. So in addition to learning that judges get pissed off about mispronunciation and long hair, I learned that it's no big deal to push beyond the rules they taught in school. There's no harm in asking. But I soon observed that I had been very conservative in my little foray outside the rules.

I had the opportunity to assist A. Frank with some of his trial work. That means that I got to do the grunt work and, as a reward, I was allowed to sit at counsel's table as he conducted the client's case. In this way I learned that it is possible to ask almost any question you can dream up and that juries (and judges) are sometimes more persuaded by the presentation of a case than by the facts (as Recht had suggested).

"Surely, Mr. Fudick, you knew that what you said was not true."

"I didn't know any such thing."

"Come, come. I put it to you, sir, that you did."

"You can 'put' whatever you want. I didn't. Are you calling me a liar?"

"Mr. Fudick, I am asking the questions."

"You're not asking questions, you're saying I'm a liar. I don't care who you are, no one calls me a liar!"

[A. Frank takes a step back, with one hand to his head and the other to his chest]. "Your honor, the witness is threatening me. I am shocked [yeah ... right] and beg the court's protection. I don't know that I can go on."

[He retreats to the table, breathing laboriously]

[The judge]: "Mr. Fudick, you have assailed the sensitive nature of counsel for the defense. I must instruct you that as a mere witness you have no standing to give offense. It is your duty to answer counsel's questions, no matter how irrelevant, intrusive, or presumptuous, and no matter what inferences as to your character may be drawn from the question or your answer. Mr. Calamari is a distinguished officer of this court. As such the court has a responsibility to care for him as if he were a child or other legally incompetent person [smiling benevolently at Mr. C.] He is only doing his job when he asks these questions. He depends for his livelihood and the needs of his family by winning cases for his clients. In this endeavor he must, since you are a witness for the plaintiff, make it appear that you are a person of mean character, low intelligence and perhaps questionable ancestry, all for the purpose of demonstrating to the jury that you should not be believed, for if the jury believes you, he has no chance of winning. If this means that he must make you out a liar, then the court must allow him to do that. This doesn't mean that you are a liar, or even a bad person. This is a legal proceeding and you mustn't take it personally. If you insist on badgering counsel, I will be forced to reprimand you most severely. Please continue Mr. Calamari."

"I am much obliged your honor. Your honor is most kind and gentle. Now, Mr. Fudick, I say that you are a liar."

"That's not a question. I say you're a fool. But since you believe me to be a liar, then you shouldn't believe that either. I lie all the time. I'm lying to you right now."

"Your honor! [retreating, holding his chest] I am overwhelmed. The witness is mocking me. I can't go on." [heavy sighs, near tears I suspect]

[The judge]: "This is too much. The witness will step down. The jury will disregard his testimony and it shall be stricken from the record."

[Opposing counsel]: "But your honor ... I object! ... your honor! This is shameful."

"Objection noted. We will take a short recess to allow Mr. Calamari to compose himself."

Recess lasted an hour and a half. A. Frank was thoroughly pleased with himself and was eager to "get back to the show."

"Isn't it true, Mr. Wedgely, that counsel for plaintiff has coached you to answer my questions by saying either "yes" or "no"?"

"Yes."

"Isn't it true, that counsel for plaintiff has instructed you to explain nothing?"

"Yes."

"Isn't it true that counsel has promised to pay you a great deal of money if you ..."

"Objection, Objection! I protest most strenuously this line of question-ing, your honor!!"

"Mr. Calamari, you know better than to imply that counsel for plaintiff may have bribed this witness."

"But what if he has, your honor?"

"Tish, tish, counselor, I'm not going to allow this. You know as well as I that the only reason witnesses show up is that they are paid to do it. You also know, though I suppose it is blasphemy to say so, that a client with enough money can find a putative expert to say whatever suits the purpose. Let us not feign *naivete*. Now get on with it."

"Your honor is most judicial. I apologize. Now, Mr. Wedgely, did you know that plaintiffs counsel graduated at the bottom of his class and took three tries to pass the bar exam, and ..."

"Your honor!! I protest most vehemently. This is chicanery. I beg the court instruct Mr. Calamari to desist!"

"Mr. Calamari, you are dangerously close to the edge. You will apologize."

"I take your point, your honor. Your honor is most fair and reasonable. I apologize to the court for disclosing that my colleague is incompetent."

"He's doing it again, your honor!! This is disgraceful!!"

"The jury will disregard Mr. Calamari's remarks."

[leaning over the table, whispering to me]: "The hell they will, kid."

It seemed to me that the jury was having great fun. They were being en-tertained by one lawyer disparaging another. They wished they had such power. Fortunately for our client (but unfortunately for the jury members, most of whom seemed to lapse into a semi-comatose condition) A. Frank ceased his more outrageous antics. Testimony dragged on for three more days. It was a complicated fact situation involving a dispute that arose out of a business transaction that the parties had attempted to memorialize, modify, amplify and qualify in a series of correspondence and other documents and in alleged oral side agreements. It was deadly dull. A. Frank knew that, and he knew that the jury, even if they understood the transaction (which they did-n't), wouldn't understand the legal consequences of finding one way or the other on the questions of fact they would be asked to resolve. His summation to the jury went something like this:

"Lady and gentlemen of the jury, you have listened with obvious interest and rapt attention to the 2 hour and 37 minute oration of my learned col-league as he struggled manfully to persuade you that his client is somehow entitled to a vast sum of money from my client. And I am compelled to say, that if you believe his version of what went on between these people, then you would be right to agree with him. But you shouldn't do that.

This is a very complicated matter and many of the facts are disputed. You have heard the officers and employees of each of the companies tell you stories that are contradictory, inconsistent and in some ways fanciful. You have heard the accountants for each company draw mutually exclusive conclusions from the same sets of numbers. You have heard "experts" flatter themselves and ridicule other "experts" on the same topics. You have seen charts which showed the intricacies of corporate ownership of other subsidiary and sister corporations with interlocking boards of directors, and organization charts which, it is asserted, show which officers or employees had what authority and who reported to whom, and god knows what else.

The sheer volume of the information and misinformation that has inundated this room has been mind numbing, and no one would fault anyone of you for not understanding what this case is about. It seems that no one has a firm grip on what actually happened or what was meant to happen under the unusual circumstances that developed ....

[The Judge]: "Surely there is an exception, Mr. Calamari."

"I was about to say 'with the exception of His Honor,' your honor."

"Continue, Mr. Calamari."

"You will be asked by his honor to answer certain questions. Your answers will determine whether my client is to suffer a most grievous hardship: the payment of a great amount of money. I will not, as my learned colleague did, try to torment the facts of this case and cast them in a light that is most favorable to my client. That would be a waste of your time and court's time. I would ask, instead, that you consider only this: you have heard all the testimony of the witnesses, you have seen all the documents, you have listened to the unrelenting monotone of plaintiff's counsel and my feeble attempts to defend my client's little business from destruction. Throughout this long ordeal I have not lied to you. Why should I? My fee doesn't depend on the outcome of this case. I'll get paid, win or lose. So I've been honest with you, and I'm being honest with you now. You should find in favor of my client, and you should do so for no other reason than because I haven't tried to dupe you. Thank you gentlemen and lady."

[The Judge]: "First, the court wishes to acknowledge its appreciation for the brevity of Mr. Calamari's summation; it is getting on toward lunch. Now, I address the Jury,

Gentlemen and lady of the jury it is my task to give you instructions and to propound to you certain questions. It is with some reluctance that I do this. From a time that the memory of man runneth not, it has been the tradition of our system of law that questions of fact are to be resolved by a group of persons chosen almost at random from the general populace.

The reasons for this are to be found in our noble and precious principles of distrust of government and our faith in the integrity, honesty and good conscience of the common man. These reasons are as valid today as they were five hundred years ago. But the simple society of that time has, alas, perished. Today, any real or imagined slight in the normal conduct of business tends to be seized upon as a cause to attempt, through the use of the courts, to extract outrageous sums of money from the alleged offender.

I sit here day after day, earning a pittance, listening to the whining of employees of multi-million, and sometimes multi-billion, dollar corporations about some dispute that could have been settled over lunch. But that is not my point. My point is that as marvelous and necessary as our jury system is, it is sometimes not up to the task that it is asked to perform.

In this case, for instance, the intricacies and complexities of the mountain of documents and the reams of testimony would tax the analytic abilities of persons of extraordinary intelligence and perspicacity. Am I supposed to overlook the obvious and pretend that each of the members of this jury is such a person? I would venture that no more than two or three of you understood all the words I used in my last two sentences. Am I to overlook the patent density of intellect demonstrated by the sleepy-eyed juryman sitting third from the left in the front row?

How, then, am I to explain the duties and propound the questions of fact in this most convoluted case in a manner that even the most bovine member of this array might understand? Shall I draw pictures?

Bailiff, I am distressed. Fetch me a bromo.

In anticipation of this point in the proceedings, and in recognition of the fact that this case has outrun the competence of this, or any other, jury, I have prepared a set of statements and questions phrased in a way which one would expect to be understood by a child. These will be given to you in writing, so that you may proceed at your own rate and focus your energy on the one word answer called for by each question, one at a time. I harbor no illusions, however, and I will be available to explain, with stick-figures if necessary, the meaning and import of any question you fail to comprehend.

[smirking] I make the same offer of assistance to counsel.

Bailiff, where is that bromo?

I trust that counsel understand the reasons for these remarks and this process. It shouldn't concern you since, as I'm sure you know, if the jury should return with any absurd result I shall send them back with instructions to find in a different way. And if I disagree with their findings as a whole I shall simply render a judgment NOV.[17] In any event, whatever the result, you boys will not be satisfied and you will find a way to continue this bit of nonsense on appeal, practically guaranteeing yourselves an annuity for the next several years, while I sit here in a state of involuntary frugality, suffering my dyspepsia."

The jury found in favor of our client. The matter was appealed on a host of points, some of which actually had merit. I wish I knew the final outcome, but I don't.

If there was a final resolution, it came long after I decided that life might be more rewarding in a corporate law department environment and had left

---

[17] *Non obstante veredicto*; that is, notwithstanding the verdict.

the firm. I'm sure I had a lot of reasons for that decision, although I can't say that I remember specifically what they were. Maybe I was uncomfortable with joining various clubs, getting involved in local politics, sitting on committees, drinking scotch with the boys: all sure-fire ways of drumming up business ("networking" in current business argot). Maybe I didn't want to learn Sicilian. Maybe the corporate environment seemed more intellectually challenging. Maybe I thought the hours would be better. Maybe I just wasn't cut out for show biz.

In any event, I don't regret a minute I spent with the firm, nor do I regret leaving it. And speaking of leaving, I think I'll leave you alone now since I've probably exceeded your attention span (just kidding; don't be so sensitive).

Our love to you and aunt Virginia.

To the Coast to Take a Meeting

Dear Uncle Fred,

I hope this finds you as well as can be expected for a person of your antiquity and temperament. Thank you for your most recent letter. I freely acknowledge that I have twisted facts and events, and related them to my children in order to cast you and Uncle Godfrey in something less than a flattering light. I did this for their entertainment and to instill in them the notion that you are much worse than I, and they should be thankful that I am as nice as I am; i.e., somewhere between Attila and Vlad the Impaler.

I hope your circumstances will come together and allow you to visit soon.

It's been a while since I've written, not because I didn't want to write, but because the flow of events has infringed on my "spare" time to the point that very little of what I prefer to do is possible of accomplishment.

When I started this letter, I was sitting in my TV room in Florida at 10:30 p.m., May 12. After spending about 2 and a half weeks back home in CT., we were compelled to return to FL due to the ill health of my father-in-law. That situation is a saga in itself, and not an uplifting one. But, dealing with unpleasant situations has been a way of life for Roberta and me for a very long time. Our kids refer to us as "crisis control." I won't bore you with specifics and I have no intention to depress you. So I will talk about something else.

A number of years ago, quite a few actually, I was a member of a squad of attorneys whose job it was to implement businessmen's decisions to buy, dissolve or sell corporate or partnership entities. This was in the days of the merger; leveraged buy-out; acquisition; make a killing without producing anything, frenzy. My client had acquired ownership of various other corporations including a homebuilder in California; commercial real estate ventures in two other states, an oil and gas service company, and interests in a couple of research, development and manufacturing partnerships. I tell you this only for the purposes of this letter, and to inform you that I spent a lot of time traveling among the various locations of those operations. Most of that travel was tedious and annoying. Occasionally, however, interesting things happened. One trip in particular stands out among that small number of those that were interesting.

The "business people" decided, for reasons almost wholly irrelevant to the purpose for which the corporation was formed (i.e., to make a profit, some of which would be distributed to shareholders) that it would be a neat thing if we were to acquire ownership interests in certain properties in Los Angeles. Those properties had recently been acquired by a reputed billionaire oil man. With that success came more debt than he cared for and he was looking to get cash by selling off pieces of the property and other assets. The properties and assets we apparently wanted included a ski resort, a golf club, overseas theater chains, and a group of bottling franchises. Why any sound minded person would want such an ill-suited mishmash of assets I couldn't tell you.

One (e.g., you) might wonder what the hell a financial services corporation would want with this motley group of assets. I know I wondered; so I asked. I don't recall the detail of the response, but its essence was that there was a felt need to diversify into non-traditional lines of business in the expectation that through such diversification the parent company's earnings would be less subject to the vagaries of the normal business cycle. The theory was that depressions in the earnings generated by that cycle could be offset by the presumed stability of earnings from the diversified group of businesses. This explanation was, of course, pure bullshit in connection with the proposed deal. It was the statement of a speculative conclusion; a hope. The fact was that we had no idea whether any of the proposed purchases were profitable under their existing management and even if they were, we didn't have a clue as to whether our management could maintain or achieve profitability. The real reason was that everyone else was diversifying and gobbling up other companies, because it was the "thing to do." It was "sexy," "now" and "it was happening."

Most of the lawyers on the team saw it the way I did, but because lawyers are reptiles we have very little higher neural function and can't see (and don't care to see) beyond our next meal. We'll do almost anything a client wants, no matter how risky, uncommonly silly, imprudent or downright stupid. After all, whatever the business outcome, we get paid.

So, on a Sunday I boarded a 747 at Bradley Field (now Bradley International in recognition of the infrequent arrival of a plane or two from outside the U.S.) and headed for Los Angeles with my friend and businessman, Bill. Bill and I had a long and friendly relationship. We had worked together on most aspects of the diversification process to that point. He was a "Director." We had made this flight many times before. Aside from a sudden, quasi-violent drop of about 500 feet (for no apparent reason) over your lovely state, which created columns of beverage over their containers before they obeyed the law of gravity and were distributed over passenger, seat and floor, it was a routine trip.

I think you would agree that seeing our country from the air is always a pleasure. I'm always taken by its colors, textures and its sheer expanse. It's beautiful. But then we descend (literally and metaphorically) toward LA. You know it's LA because the layer of air that sits on it is a series of sickeningly hued strata ranging from an opaque yellow to a malevolent beige-gray. People in LA actually breathe that filth all day, every day. The city itself is everywhere and nowhere. It is spread for miles up and down the coast with no discernible center or hub. This is as it should be. The people, like their city, sprawl out in any direction with no lynch pin (of philosophy, principle, tradition, or other standard of behavior) to fetter their wanderings. It is the land of the Lotus Eaters.

Bill and I picked up the papers for our rental car, found the car and headed into the City. Bill drove. I took a look at the papers as he drove.

"How many miles does this thing have on it?"

"'Bout 9,000."

"Funny. It's supposed to have 12,400. What kind of car is this?"

"It's a Mercury."

"More funny. It's supposed to be a Ford. Jezzus-chrise, we've got the wrong car."

"Piss on it, [says Bill]. I'm not going back."

I agreed. What difference would it make which of Mr. Hertz' cars we had?

We were greeted at the hotel by a bozo in a beefeater costume who arranged to have other, more conventionally, uniformed attendants carry our bags inside and take away Mr. Hertz' car to the underground parking area. The hotel would be the place to wash, change and sleep for the week, while most of our waking hours would be spent about a mile away at the office. That evening we met other lawyers and business people and discussed the rules of engagement for the next day. A fellow named Rolf was the lead business person and he would be point man.

My assignment was "due diligence" which means that it was my responsibility to check facts, assertions of fact, ferret out inconsistencies and determine whether what the other side was saying about their potential legal exposures was true. It is necessary to do this because in the American system of jurisprudence, there is no requirement that the parties to an anticipated agreement negotiate in good faith. In other words, there are no legal sanctions for lying and cheating before an agreement is signed. At signing, the duty of good faith springs like Athena from the head of Zeus to compel the parties, who to this point have been doing their utmost to hoodwink, scam, con and fleece each other, to behave like choir boys. By that time, however, it is usually too late as a practical matter to avoid lengthy and expensive efforts to rectify prior missteps, mistakes, oversights or chicanery. It's better to find out for yourself than rely on anything they say during negotiations.

Bill and I decided to walk the one-mile to the office. The first two days were spent in analyzing litigation in process, pending or threatened; reviewing liabilities accrued and anticipated for compensation, benefits, state mandated payments and a host of other similarly uninteresting but necessary tasks. These sessions went from 8 in the morning to 9 or 10 at night, and were enough to deaden the spirit of even the most enthusiastic participant. But I know my job and I know how to do it, even when it makes me want to puke. My job is to be an unmitigated thorn in the side, burr under the saddle, pain in the ass. I am well suited to this function, particularly when I'm not having a good time. I established myself as a non-Californian early on.

"I want to see all the employment litigation files. Everything you've got on age, race, and sex discrimination charges; any and all employee complaints and all union disputes."

"You can't be serious; there are hundreds of them."

"I assure you that I am totally serious and that I want them ASAP. I also want a complete accounting of your litigation expenses for the last three years and your projection of such expenses for the next fiscal year."

"OK, if that's what you want I'll see what I can do. But that's a lot of work."

"Let me worry about that. There's a lot of money at stake and I will find out how much of it is going to take to clean up the mess you guys are in."

How's that for being pompous, overbearing and rude? Many people think I'm really like that. Hey. So be it. I ain't no freakin' monument to Judeo-Christian civility. I'm a lawyer for chrise sake.

On Wednesday, we were to meet with the billionaire man himself. He was a big guy; tall and wide, almost fat. His clothes were obviously expensive but didn't seem to hang right. He sounded like an oil guy; personable and folksy; talked about his kids with affection, and projected that just-a-country-boy image. When we left the meeting, Rolf said, "So what do you think?" "Hide the silverware," I said.

We then went on an informal tour of the property guided by a guy who had been there for 20 or so years. He pointed out the various features and history of the site, indicating that it would "really" be "like" a "total" shame to demolish all this history, warmth, nostalgia, etc., and indicating that such demolition would bring "bad Karma." Bill nodded and muttered his assent to these statements, paused and said, "OK, Mario, bring in the bulldozers. Ha ha ha ha." The guy didn't laugh. He knew that one of the "concepts" for the property was the removal of all that "history" and the creation of a group of horrendously expensive "executive condominiums." After all, when the likes of Gerald Ford and your old buddy Henry Kissinger had expressed an interest in investing in such over-priced ostentation, history be damned, we're talking progress here; we're talking megabucks, we're talking pizzazz, now, jacuzzis all-round, Porsche in every garage; hey, we're talking the advance of Western civilization! Who was I to say no?

On Thursday, events took an unexpected turn. To that point I had been working double shifts, operating on a few hours sleep and a diet of coffee, cigarettes, pizza, Chinese and KFC. The result was that I was ahead of sched-

schedule and looking forward to some rest on Friday. Thursday morning, I got a call from a senior executive of our homebuilder, the main office of which was down south, near the Santa Anna airport (now "Duke" after the late, great John Wayne). He asked that I come down, if at all possible, to terminate the employment of a management guy who had been accused of certain improprieties (mostly either unproved or not provable) with respect to corporate property (the word "property" being defined broadly to include certain female staff members). I told him that while I had a full day ahead of me, I would be able to come down Friday morning - we could talk about it then. He thanked me. I hung up and went to meet Bill.

It was raining. We decided to forgo our usual walk and asked the beef-eater guy to get our car. "No problem, sir, be right here." We waited. No car. The car guy appeared on foot. He spoke into the ear of the beefeater guy.

The beefeater guy said to Bill, "We can't seem to locate your car. Would you go with Lance [Lance??] to identify it?" Bill said sure; got into another car and drove off into the dank bowels of the hotel foundation that doubled as the secured parking area. I waited. No car. No Bill. No Lance [Lance!?]

I went over to the beefeater guy, who was standing with his eyes closed humming what I presumed to be his guru-recommended mantra, and asked him what was going on. He kept his eyes shut, interrupted his chant and said in the laid-back, mellow tones of the Lotus Eater:

"That car is in Tiajuana being painted a different color as we speak, man. No big thing, just part of the cosmic plan for redistribution of the things of the earth."

There you have it. The cosmic plan called for the theft of a goddam rental car - my rental car. How wonderful is the cosmic consciousness. It is so omnipotent that it can ordain the theft of a rental car, located on the west coast of a continent on a tiny hunk of dirt and water, circling around a nonde-script star, plodding in a spiral arm backwater of a galaxy of billions of stars, the entire galaxy forming but an infinitesimal part of a universe of billions of galaxies, each rushing away from each other at tens of thousands of miles an hour. What an asshole!

I stood next to him, closed my eyes and hummed Camptown Races. I had to; it was in the cosmic plan.

Bill returned. No car. Hertz had an office in the hotel. We went in. A comely young woman with a plastic smile and feathered earrings asked if she could help us. Well, maybe, and maybe not. The paperwork was in the car, and even if we had it, it wasn't the car the paperwork said it was; but we needed a car anyway. We explained all that as her plastic smile became tighter at the corners, her eyes shifted from us to a corner of the room, and she made what I can only describe as clucking sounds which seemed to ema-nate from her throat, as if she were some demented ventriloquist whose chicken puppet had disappeared. "I'll have to get the manager," she said. She did. We went through our tale. The manager made no reference to a cosmic plan. He did, however, refer to a computer contraption on the desk and was able to confirm that we did indeed have (at one time at least) a car assigned to us. He concluded "No problem. I'll have another brought up."

The car he had brought up was an AMC Concorde with 11 miles on the odometer. I checked the papers; they matched the car. We were now an hour late. Bill was driving. I said,

"You smell something?"

"Like what?"

"Like something burning?"

"Yeah. I think it's that piece of shit Pinto in front of us."

We pulled into the office security checkpoint and stopped to get parking clearance. Bill told the guard who we were and who we were meeting. The guard calmly asked,

"Is it of any concern to you, sir, that your car is on fire?"

Smoke was now wafting from under the hood. It smelled electrical. Bill demanded, "Where can I put it?" The guard pointed and calmly directed, "Put it over there." We got it over there and bailed out. "Whaddawe do now," I said. "Hell with it, let it burn, we're late," said Bill. We went to work, leaving the Concorde to the intentions of the cosmic consciousness.

When we left the building that night the Concorde was still sitting there, unconsumed. We got in it, Bill at the wheel, drove to the security booth where we were stopped and informed that we had parked in an unauthorized spot and would have to pay a fine of some $25. Bill looked at the piece of paper the guard had thrust at him. He handed it back saying, "I ain't paying a fine." The guard said, "You got it." Bill said, "No, I don't, you do," as he nailed the throttle and peeled out of the driveway. Smoke followed us to hotel; acrid aromas filled the car. A guy in a beefeater costume hastily absented himself as we pulled in. We parked in front of the Hertz window and went in. They had seen us drive up. The same crew was still there. The plastic smile was not in evidence. She said nothing, staring at the manager, who was staring out the window, enthralled by the plumes of oily, black smoke that were rolling out the back of the hood and up the windshield. Camptown racers sing this song ...

He said nothing, punching keys on that computer thing. Pause ...buzzz...whirrrr. Shuffle. He pushed an envelope and some keys in front of Bill. I got to them first. "He's jinxed," I said. "I'll take over from here." No one had said a word 'til then, and no one spoke thereafter. Do da, do da......

We went to our rooms, met an hour later and walked to a restaurant. Several others of the team joined us. Some of them were clearly "into it." It was their first exposure to Caliphoney. They were having a wonderful time in LaLa land, wheeling and dealing, utilizing the dealmaker's buzzwords, interspersing Caliphoney-speak expressions and generally reveling in being at the cutting edge of a cultural, socio-economic happening. What a bunch of addle-headed shit! We were wasting tens of thousands of shareholder dollars in an endeavor that would ultimately cost them millions more. I couldn't wait to get down south to take some names and kick some ass. At least they were making money down south, the only reason for their existence as far as I was concerned. I hoped the guy I was going to fire was a native Caliphonian.

Bill and I left LaLa early Friday in a Buick Regal, having received a sing-song farewell benediction from the beefeater guy which I heard as, "May the sun shine on you." and Bill heard as, "Have your shoe shined too." Whatever. I drove. The cosmic plan apparently called for no further automobile related events. I should give you some of the context for what follows.

A number of years earlier, we had entered into a partnership that engaged in large-scale residential and commercial real estate development. For various reasons, most having to do with the failure of our business people to maintain adequate management and accounting controls over the partnership, the arrangement proved unsatisfactory (i.e., we weren't making money). The partners agreed, in essence, to split the assets and dissolve the partnership; a process that took a year and a half to accomplish. That process cost the partners hundreds of thousands of dollars in attorney fees, but at least it kept the attorneys for both sides focused on each other, something relatively harmless to society at large.

One of the pieces we took was the homebuilder I mentioned earlier. As an outgrowth of my work on the partnership dissolution, I had been retained as counsel, for certain limited purposes, by the homebuilder. In that capacity, I sometimes had the task of telling people that their services were no longer required. This didn't happen often, but with enough frequency that the people there had begun to feel that whenever I arrived someone (or more) would be fired.

The company sponsored "attitude adjustment parties" as they were called. People from the corporate office would get together after hours to eat and drink (mostly drink). The object of these festivities was the creation of an atmosphere of camaraderie, relaxation and good fellowship, all toward the end of fostering "team spirit" in the hope that they would be more productive. At one of these excuses to deplete corporate assets, a person I did not know approached me and in the slurred speech of an inebriate informed me, "I know you. You're that guy. Ya know what we call you? ... Huh? Do ya know what we call you? ... We call you the Assassin. You - hic - bastard." Well, I know now.

So it wasn't unusual for me to handle terminations. Management liked it because they had to go on managing the survivors and they could do that more easily if they could point at me as the bad guy and claim they had no hand in the matter. So be it. I don't care whether people do what they should out of love or out of fear, as long as they do it. Obviously, love as motivation is preferable, but failing that, I'll take the other end of the spectrum over something in the neutral, wishy-washy middle.

Now, with respect to that person I was assigned to terminate, it appeared that there was some evidence to support allegations of preferential treatment toward certain members of his staff. It would also appear to a jaundiced eye that that treatment was granted on the basis of participation in extra-office activities rather than business related, meritorious work performance. Keep in mind that this was years ago, during the latter stages of the "dawning of the age of Aquarius," casual sex, and the whatever-it-takes mode of attaining material wants.

The horrors of avaricious lawyers beating the drums of litigation over every real or imagined reference to gender, no matter how trivial, as sexual harassment, and the current perception of sex, with anyone, as a *molto pericoloso*,[18] possibly deadly, game of Russian roulette, were outside the scope of awareness of even the most prescient observer of the then social scene. I was not then, and am not now, a moralist. I think everyone should do whatever it is they want to do, and they are free to do so without any let or hindrance from me. I think that the entire population of this globe can go to hell in a hand basket if that's what it wants. In fact (although only a few years ago I rejected this view as too harsh) I am becoming more convinced as the evidence keeps piling up, that the human race is so stupid and venal that it isn't worth saving, and if there is such a thing as a cosmic consciousness, it should spit every last member of the species into the utmost depths of the abyss. But I digress.

The allegations, in general, were that this guy was dipping his pen in the company ink, so to speak. I spoke with the informants and the persons allegedly favored. I read the files on those persons and persons similarly situated, comparing particularly the performance evaluations of the "favored" versus those not favored and the compensation and other employment related factors pertinent to each group. My assessment was that there was enough evidence to make at least a *prima facia*[19] case that there had been extra-office relationships that might have had the effect of influencing the grant of unwarranted favor on the participants through the use, directly or indirectly, of company assets.

As I said, I'm not in the habit of making moral judgments. Law and morality are not the same thing. I couldn't care less that this guy was boinking the help. I did care, however, that a member of company management had not only exercised poor judgment in the first instance, but had compounded his folly by abusing his managerial authority in favoring his paramours, thus causing disruption, discontent and resentment within his own department. This stupidity seriously impaired his standing to do his job and caused senior management to lose faith in his capacity to adequately perform the duties of his position (or, being translated, if he's stupid enough to pull shit like this, what other stupid shit has he pulled, or will he pull?).

---

[18] Very dangerous
[19] At first sight.

100

I went to his office. He said he wasn't surprised to see me. I advised him that he no longer had a job; that I would give him an hour to clean out his desk; that I would take his keys, credit card and security pass. He asked if I was going to fire "the girls." I told him they would not be terminated. He asked why not. I said, "Because they're not stupid." "Suppose I got a lawyer?" he asked. "That's your prerogative," I said, "but what do you suppose your spouse's reaction will be?" "I'll be out of here in a half hour," he said. "I'll wait," said I. "You're a cold-hearted bastard," he muttered.

Camptown racetrack five miles long ....

I escorted him to the door. He didn't look back. As I went back through the office conversations ceased, doors closed, an uneasy silence moved ahead of and followed behind me. Assassin, huh? Could be worse I suppose. With that bit of mischief done, I reported back to senior management and we went on to other matters.

The office staff had been trying to get Bill and me a room for the night, but they were coming up empty. Even the nearest Motel 6 was saying they couldn't assure us a room when we got there. Great. We're supposed to leave tomorrow, we gave up our rooms at the LaLa hotel. Maybe we'll sleep in the car. One of the office managers - "Human Resources" manager - came to our rescue. She said she was having a few people over tonight at her new place, which had three bedrooms. We were welcome to come over for dinner and stay the night. We accepted. She gave us directions. I drove.

The Newport Beach area of southern Caliphoney is about midway between LaLa and San Diego. At that time it was experiencing a tremendous growth spurt. Land once used to graze cattle and grow avocados was being mercilessly bulldozed to make way for office buildings, malls, condos, gas stations, etc. The hills, previously capable only of supporting scrub and a few trees, were reworked to support overblown and outrageously priced single family homes. America! What a country! Our directions led us through some low hills heavily laden with condo complexes. Each set tried to be different, cute, quaint or distinctive in some way from each other set. But within each set there was, despite the efforts at variation, a monotonous uniformity, like army barracks, but barracks on LSD. The complex we were after had that uniformity but was distinguishable from others by reason of its odd admixture of gothic, Victorian and south-west motif; sort of a medieval-American-architectural nightmare rendered into reality by the folks at Disney.

Our hostess greeted us and introduced her "significant other/life partner" of the moment. His name was Bob, and he took us on a tour of the house while the lady busied herself with dinner preparations. The house was surprisingly well planned and implemented, with copious living area provided at the expense of tiny bedrooms. All in all, it was very nice.

Bob gave us a continuous commentary on the home's special or unique features, spending much time explaining the components, operation, advantages and disadvantages of his leading edge, custom designed, top of the line, security system. It was everywhere and it did everything. If a field mouse had the temerity to attempt entry into Bob's domain, Bob would know about it. Moreover, both cars in the vault-like garage were themselves equipped with similar leading edge, etc., technological marvels and as if that weren't enough, he also possessed that apex of security devices, a .357 Magnum.

This last bit of equipment was kept in his bedroom, except when he went out into the hills to practice his marksmanship by blowing spiders out of their webs and into oblivion. Bob was, not to put too fine a point on it, a fruitcake whose vocation, backed by several degrees from prestigious institutions of higher learning, was counseling other fruitcakes on how to deal with and overcome their insecurities. I concluded that Bob either had no, or a very small, penis.

Dinner guests arrived. Intros all around. Yak, yak, yak; get to know you; ain't Caliphoney grand; just bought this or that; my BMW; my Porsche; make a million; to the mountains; Catalina; blah, blah. Typical question; "What's your role?" My response: "Sesame seed." Another: "What's your sign?" My response: "No thru trucks."

Please, cosmic consciousness, get the goddam food on the table so these yammering yahoos will shut up. The guests were no doubt good people, yet I had the sense of being in the presence of the more flighty members of the population of the enchanted forest. First food, then drink.

Lotsa drink. Lotsa "security"; .357; BMW , etc. ... I hear someone mention an air traffic controllers strike.

WHAT?! Maybe tomorrow? *Merde*! When did you hear that? Damn! Is it on? Maybe tomorrow.

Bill and I decide we best get up real early, get to LAX and try to get home. The guests, but for one, depart. The "one" has had a drop too many of drink and our host and hostess demand (quite rightly) that she not drive, but sleep it off here. Bill and I can bunk in one room. She can have the other. No problem. Do da, do da.

We say goodnight and goodbye, thanking our hosts and promising that we won't wake them when we leave at 5 a.m. At 3 a.m. our fellow guest awakens, still besotted and totally *divestude*. Dazed and confused, thought blurred by alcohol but fearful of the, by now notorious, security system, she creeps in the gloom searching for the bathroom. Finding a door she believes leads to the object of her desire, she opens it and steps in, groping for a light switch. She finds it as the door closes behind her. The burst of light reveals that she is in the garage. She turns back to the door, clutches the knob only to find it is locked. Naked, befuddled and cold, she doesn't dare pound on the door or attempt to get into one of the cars; an alarm will wake the household, summon the police and bring out the .357. She elects to lie down on the floor.

At 5, Bill's watch alarm goes off. I hear it, uncramp myself from the sofa, and shake Bill awake. We gather our stuff, go down to the kitchen, quietly have some coffee, grab some food out of the refrigerator and sneak out the front door being careful not to set off the alarm. The lady in the garage hears the front door shut; hears us start our Buick Regal and leave. She lies back down.

We drop Mr. Hertz' car off and head into LAX. The air traffic controllers' strike is on. Our flight is cancelled. The place is in an uproar. We tell the person at the desk we want to head east, anywhere east. At about 8:30 we're called. They have room on a flight to Phoenix.

At about the same time, Bob opens the door to the garage and recoils at the shocking, yet perversely delightful, sight of a naked woman lying on the cement floor of his garage, like a sacrificial maiden being offered to the grille of his beloved Porsche. In his shock, he pitches backward, losing his grip on his golf bag, which crashes into the aquarium. Water and fish fly with the shattered glass. The water causes a short in a nearby electrical outlet, actuating the alarm that will bring the police and fire departments (along with a legion of neighbors). The sleeping nude jumps up screaming like a demonic Venus Rising. The Human Resources manager, awakened by the clamor of alarm and scream, grabs the .357 and charges into the hall.

Bill and I get on the plane to Phoenix. By the time we land, the situation in Caliphoney has been resolved. Bob has decided to sell the .357 and suggested that his significant other/life partner of the moment go to jazzercise. Bill and I spend 5 hours in Phoenix and arrange a flight to Dallas/Fort Worth. Later we get to Chicago, then to Atlanta, and finally to Boston. We rent a car in Boston. I drive home and turn the car over to Bill.

It is now Sunday afternoon. Roberta seems mildly pleased to see me. The kids take no notice of my arrival. Roberta asks about the trip. I tell her it was interesting, and as I give her a synopsis of the past 36 hours, Bill has a blowout, veers off the road and crunches Mr. Hertz' car. I haven't rented a Hertz car since. I know the cosmic plan when I see it.

I bet my money on a bobtail nag ...

Well, I think I've caused you enough fatigue for a while, so I'm going to print this out and send it off. Please take care of yourself and give my love to Aunt Virginia. If you've been in contact with the crew in Rhode Island, don't believe everything you hear, OK?

The Road to Harrisburg

Dear Uncle Fred,

R oberta and I recently completed a 2,500 mile round-trip to our place in Florida. Our route is primarily interstate highway 95, one of the most heavily traveled roads in the country (and, incidentally, the chief corridor for the movement of illicit drugs between Florida and New York/New England). Driving time for the trip is about 23 hours, depending on road conditions and traffic, which is almost always a frustrating experience from the Garden State, along the Jersey pike to 295 to 95, through Baltimore, the D.C inner loop and the black hole of Alexandria Va.

The traffic volume decreases after Richmond and doesn't bottle up again until Jacksonville. Why the best engineers the world has ever produced saw fit to place a major interstate across two bodies of water to have it pass over an island, I will never know, but I suppose there are other more weird things in the world. Anyway, the trip was virtually uneventful (a rarity).

On the way through North Carolina, we traveled for an hour or so with a group of tractor trailers, which were running in a "convoy." Traveling with such a group has advantages. You can move at the maximum possible speed - well in excess of the posted limit - and if some mishap or police activity should lie in wait, the entire column, like an integrated consciousness, slows down to evade problems or responsibility. It was during this communal trekking that I asked Roberta if she ever missed trucking. She said that she did, but not very much, and would be giving up her class 1 license when it came up for renewal. She asked the same of me, and I replied in the same way. All this is simply an introduction to the story I'm about to tell you. There are a number of trucking stories I could relate, but I think this one will suffice to illustrate our perspective.

In 1942, Roberta's father (Robert) was asked to perform certain services for our country. He agreed and spent several years enjoying the scenery and people of Europe, meeting the natives of Italy, France and Germany. While he doesn't talk very much about his sojourn there, we assume that he had a nice time. During this period he had the opportunity to practice the skills the army had taught him. However, as you well know, post '45 there was little call for BAR, grenade tossing, claymore wiring, and like experience in civil-

105

ian life.[20] Robert became a truck driver, an occupation that he would pursue for the following 38 years, proudly displaying the insignia of Teamsters Local 251.

With this influence in her early years, Roberta retained the notion that someday she would become a truck driver. Not a person easily diverted from fulfilling her wants, about 12 years ago she bought two International Transtar tractors (cab-over), equipped with Detroit 318 diesels, 13 speed Fuller transmissions, 12,000 lbs. front axles, and 38,000 lbs. twin rear axles.[21] She also acquired two 45' flat bed trailers, because it was her intent to haul steel and similar bulk loads that are typically loaded and unloaded by means of over-head cranes. At about the same time, our son-in-law, Jeffrey, was living his childhood dream as an owner-operator of his Peterbilt (conventional), hauling whatever needed to be hauled.

My part in Roberta's business (PKL, Inc.) was that of mechanic, consultant (mostly mechanic) and spare driver. I had learned to drive when I was a teenager, under the tutelage of Roberta's father, on a beastly Autocar. Roberta had several drivers, depending on business need, including her father and Jeffrey. Jeff helped her out; she helped him out. This meant that on occasion I worked on Jeff's truck or shared driving duty on his trips.

It was a Monday. I received a call from Roberta at 2:15. She told me that Jeff had agreed to take his truck to the vicinity of Harrisburg to pick up a trailer that had been loaded with spools of telephone cable. But Jeff had just returned from a trip and was tired; would I go with him? I said no; but when I say no, my decision is subject to my spouse's veto, under some sort of constitutionally granted superior power. It's like the legislative process. I gather information, assess the needs and wants of our clan, balance those needs and

---

[20] "BAR" is abbreviation of Browning automatic rifle, a "light" machine gun.
"Claymore" is an anti-personnel explosive, set about waist high and activated by trip wire.
[21] The 318 refers to horsepower, not cubic inch displacement. The rears in trucker talk are "twin screws."

wants against the common welfare of the clan, its individual members, financial and fiscal opportunities and restraints, and make a decision in the form of a declaration of policy.

As thoroughly reasoned as that declaration may be, as urgent, necessary or appropriate it may be, it is subject to veto and, in this context, reversal by Roberta (or the wishes of one of my three daughters). In this family, male members have no final decision-making power. Their role is confined to tentative conclusions only. In any event, my "no" decision was vetoed and reversed before I got home. I was informed of this about-face by Darlene (aka "Dolly") when she said, "Daddy, please don't let Jeff go alone tonight." I know a veto when I hear one.

Lacking power to override the veto, I had supper, filled the thermos with coffee, and at about 7:30 in the evening climbed into the Peterbilt with Jeff and headed toward Harrisburg. Jeff's Peterbilt was an old one. Actually, it was an old two. Several years before, he had bought two tractors, each of which, in itself, was incapable of meeting road-worthiness standards. However, through a combination of their parts and the judicious application of some new parts, we succeeded in creating one serviceable vehicle. That hybrid would sometimes require ad hoc modification, as this trip would demonstrate.

I was driving, heading southwest, somewhere near Scranton, when a light snow began to dust the road. This was not a good thing. We were running bobtail, which means that the twin-screw rear, designed to withstand a 38,000 lbs. load, had nothing but the chassis and the fifth wheel above it; not enough weight to hold it on the road continuously. With the rears sometimes in the air, traction is hard to come by, and with the weight on the front wheels the horse wants to slide sideways in turns. Under these circumstances I kicked it down a few notches and we were moving at about 35 mph when the lights went out. They were out for about 5 seconds, then on again. An aberration, I thought. No. A minute later, off again, this time for about 30 seconds. After a brief period of renewed illumination, they went off and stayed off.

I kept moving, put on the hazards (they worked) and used what light was available from the running lights (five on the cab roof and one on each fender) to align myself between the broken lane divider and the solid shoulder marker, both of which were in the process of being disappeared under the shifting sheets of snow. Jeff and I were not silent, of course. We discussed our options and decided that since we were within a few miles of a truck stop, we'd press on.

It got surrealistic. The running lights are yellow. Under normal circumstances the effect is a golden glow that gives a feeling of comfort. The white of the head lights cuts through the black in front and the running lights blend the whiteness gently back to the black as it moves past the cab. Now there was only the soft glow of the dash instruments and the golden glow became a ball of murky beige as it vainly fought against the black which was now aided by the swirling flakes in cutting us off from whatever reality lay ahead. I shut down the dash lights. Now the black invaded the cab except for the periodic blink of the hazard flash indicator.

A Detroit engine makes a distinctive sound. It's a two-cycle engine, and with all that displacement (about 850 cubic inches) the sound it produces, when pushed through twin stacks, is an unmistakable snarl. The snarl now seemed louder than it should be. Jeff and I did not speak; he was relying on my skill and judgment, and I was relying on his young eyes to alert me to any imminent danger and the longed for exit ramp.

"I got a sign!" [Jeff's voice was a bit higher than normal.]

"Is it a sign from god? And if it is I hope it says electrical contractor."

"You asshole. The exit's a mile ahead."

A sign from god if I ever saw one. It was a slow mile, but we got it behind us and pulled into a well-lighted parking lot. We checked connections in the cab. Nothing. We went out into the snow and after some difficulty in raising the monstrous hood, began checking lines. Nothing. While we were monkeying around, the lights flickered on at random intervals, but there seemed to be no connection (no pun intended) between what we were checking and the flickering.

Jeff figured it out. Every time we nudged the hood against the chassis the lights came on. We had a bad ground. Rather than find and fix it, we rigged a piece of wire between the hood and the chassis. That did it. We got back on the road; a long, slow road. Jeff drove because the loss of my adrenalin high had left me in something less than the best condition to drive.

At 3 in the morning (3 hours late) we arrived at a truck stop within a few miles of our destination. I needed a coffee (the quantity in the thermos had been consumed) and a pack of cigarettes (I was running low). I was intent on replenishing the supply of these, my drugs of preference, when Jeff announced that he was "...going to call that guy."

"Christ, Jeff, it's 3 o'clock. He's gone home by now, or if he hasn't he's probably pissed off."

"Don't give a shit."

I let him go; I had more important things to do.

"That guy" was still there waiting for us when Jeff called. He said to come over. We did. It was still snowing. The road wasn't ploughed or sanded, but there was only 3 inches or so on the road, and we were confident that our jerry-rigged ground wire would hold out. I don't know what I was expecting; perhaps I expected a terminal of some sort, with lights and a paved yard; perhaps a warehouse with some loading docks; or maybe a big garage with other trucks around. What I got was a small, short, snow-covered driveway leading to a house trailer, behind which was a large area cleared in the surrounding trees, with no lights, no trucks, no garage, no docks - just some scattered remains of mechanical

108

things and a 40' flat bed trailer to which four huge spools of cable had been lashed with chains and binders. Okay, okay, no big deal, we just back under the trailer, hook-up, pull up the dolly and we're off.

Yeah, right.

"That guy" was Emile. Emile looked about 50; hadn't shaved in a few days; stood about 5' 9" and weighed somewhere around 225 lbs. He wore a plaid shirt under a ruined parka that was opened in its entirety, thus disclosing the plaid shirt, which in turn was open at the top. The shirt was also open at the bottom, but unlike the top (which I assumed was open intentionally) the bottom was open by reason of the location of a good portion of the 225 lbs. at about what would ordinarily be the belt line. The belt line in this instance was at crotch level, and caused by the mass of cellulite above attempting to obey the law of gravity. The distance between the last buttoned hole of the shirt and the crotch was covered by the lower portion of a white T shirt, which had obviously been subject to the elements for some time.

"Hey you boys. Took ya' a while to get here, eh?"

"Yeah, yeah, pain in the ass. Sorry we're late."

"No problem, got nuthin' else to do. You boys want a drink?"

3:30 A.M. is not my normal drinking hour, so we declined with thanks and asked Emile for the bill of lading.

"Got no bill," said Emile. "Alls I got is this paper that says who it's from and where it's goin'. You can have that. [So much for formalities.] Yup, that rig's been sittin' there for a month. Old boy that dropped it here couldn't go no further. That's what's left of his tractor over there. [He pointed to an unidentifiable mass out there in the dark.]

Old boy said his boss wasn't payin' 'im, and the truck was shit. Har, har, har. So he stayed here for three days pullin' it apart and sellin' the parts to anybody that wanted 'em. Hee, hee. Boy, some people. Hee, hee, hee. But no business of mine. People do what they wanna do, … ya' know?"

Do people actually get to do what they want to do?

Jeff wasn't in a mood to discuss people's liberties. He wanted out of there; a want I shared. He backed up to the trailer, but that's all. The weight of the load on the small surface of the dolly plates had, over the prior month of freezing and thawing, driven them down into the dirt. This decrease in elevation made the tractor too high to slide the fifth wheel under the trailer. Shouldn't be a problem; just crank down the dolly. The dolly was fully extended; that alternative wasn't available.

Okay, now what? Jeff opined, and I concurred, that our only course was to lower the tractor. This we did by letting some of the air out of the tractor tires (not a drastic step because we could inflate the tires from the compressor which is an essential and standard component of the tractor). Jeff tried to ease his way under the trailer. No go. We let more air out. Try again. Almost, but now we're seriously under inflated and to the point of damaging all eight rear tires. Alternative? Ram the bastard!

Two rams and the fifth wheel shrieked its way under the trailer and caught the pin. This is a good thing. We make the electrical connection with no untoward incident, but find that the "glad-hand" (the connecting device that links the tractor's air supply to the trailer) is not of the same manufacture as the corresponding hand affixed to the trailer lines. Only three companies manufacture these devices and 90% of those in use are compatible, but not these two. Jeff takes the initiative and through the use of simple hand tools modifies the offending hand to conform to the demands of the occasion. This is also a good thing, but the dollies are still frozen in the ground.

Using our heads, we reason that re-inflating the tires will break the dollies free. We re-inflate to 94 psi (standard pressure) but the effect is somewhat different from anticipated. The dollies remain imbedded in the ground and the front end of the tractor isn't touching same. The time has come to abandon the head's reasoning and resort to instinct. I go to the trailer and ask Emile if he has a sledge hammer. He does - a 12 pounder. I crawl under the trailer, and assuming a semi-squat position virtually certain to produce an intestinal aneurysm, I tell Jeff to try rocking the rig.

As he tries rocking, particles of sand and fragments of stone spit past me from the churning, growling tires. I wail the bejezzus out of a dolly strut. Miraculously it breaks loose, the combined freedom from the restraint below, the abrupt equalization of the relative levels of tractor and trailer, and the force of the 318 horses from the angry Detroit, release untold mega thousands of ergs that result in a lurch that causes the other dolly to explode from its subterranean trap and move the entire rig upward and forward by 1 foot and 3 feet respectively. Still on instinct, I launch myself sideways, landing on my back, skidding on the wet snow, grasping the sledge hammer as if it could somehow protect me. Jeff jumps from the now quiet horse yelling, "Holy shit, what was that!?" "Success," I say (but too soon).

"I'll pull it ahead so we can check out the lights 'n stuff," Jeff says. Sure.

He fires it up; the engine whines; I hear the universal take up the strain; the engine revs higher. The rig begins to move, but clearly something is amiss. Too little motion is being produced by too much energy. Jeff again jumps out. He's muttering emphatically

"What the fug?? Jessuz christ! Jessuz sufferin' chrise!"

"Jeff, I think the rear brakes are frozen, the tires aren't turning; you were dragging them."

"Sufferin' chrise, goddammit, shit, bastard! [says Jeff] Sonofabitch, bastard, shit."

He seems upset, so in my best fatherly voice I attempt to bring, as a good parent should (and I was, after all, in *loco parentis* at this juncture) some perspective and balance to the situation; something that doesn't come easily to me, especially at 5 in the morning, in the cold, the dark, and the snow, 6 hours from home. I say,

"Jeffrey, Jeffrey, Jeffrey. Life can be an adventure or an ordeal; it's all in what you make of it."

"Screw that shit. Where's that flippin' sledge hammer."

Sometimes the fatherly approach doesn't produce the intended result.

We crawl under the trailer. I don't know how much you know about these things so let me explain the parking brake system on a tractor-trailer. As I said, an air compressor is standard equipment; in fact, it is essential. It's essential because the brakes are operated by compressed air. You may recall being near a rig when it was being parked. That loud release of air you heard was the driver actuating the "maxies." What happens is roughly this: air pressure is removed from pneumatic cylinders attached to the braking mechanism within the hubs on which the tires are mounted. When that happens, sturdy steel springs, hitherto under compression, push the brake shoes out against the inside of the hubs. With no air pressure the brakes are fully on.

Of course, while the trailer was sitting there for a month, there was no pressure and under the climatic conditions during that period the brakes had become glued, so to speak, to the hubs. The air pressure we put back into the system when we hooked up was insufficient to break the union. Sufficient power would now be applied through the principles pertinent to motion, mass and Newton's laws. In other words, we beat up the brakes. They all released after brief periods of concentrated persuasion.

"Jeff? Do you hear an air leak?"

"Yeah, I do. Where's it coming from?"

"I don't know."

"Check the lines."

"Judas priest!! It's not a line. We've got a tire going flat!" [At this point life was approximating an ordeal. I heard a rooster crowing.]

"Hey you boys. [Emile's voice] You boys still playin?" [Does that guy sleep?]

"Yeah [says Jeff, trying to imitate Emile's accent] we got us a bad tahre."

"No problem. [says Emile] Ah'll fix you up with another one."

I think: now here's a sign from god. Maybe "mechanic on duty." Jeff and Emile disappear into the gloom from which Emile would produce another "tahre." I check out lights, lines, hoses, etc. and am headed for the cab to get warm when I hear Jeff:

"Hey, you boy, we gotta put this here tahre on."

Bloody goddam marvelous.

We jacked up the axle, pulled the lug nuts, pulled the tire, mounted the other, reset the lug nuts, let the jack down, stowed all our gear, returned Emile's gear, fired her up and headed for the highway home. It was now about 7. Black was slowly giving way to gray. Snow steadily layered everything. The road seemed fairly navigable. It would be safer now that we had some weight over the screws. Jeff said he was awake. The cab was warm. I pulled my collar up, pushed back in the seat and rested by eyes.

I was in a plane. The engines were changing pitch. Emile was in a captain's uniform with the dirty lower end of his T shirt sticking out of his jacket, saying "Hey you boys, put your seat in a full upright position." I shook it off in fright; unrested my eyes to discern that the engine had indeed changed pitch and that we were pulling off the road. It was still snowing and the road had become less hospitable. It was now 9:30 and I asked Jeff, "What's up?" "I gotta get out from behind the wheel," he said.

Had I been more awake myself I would have pointed out to him the grammatical impropriety of stringing prepositions together like that, but no matter. He had had a long night. I took over, somewhat groggy, and asked Jeff what he wanted to do. That might seem a terribly non-specific inquiry, but in this context Jeff knew what I meant. He said, "Just drive. I want to get home. The guys coming south say it's better ahead."

He had been talking on the CB with drivers who had come through New York. When Jeff drives he usually has the CB and either the radio or the tape deck going. Because I can't stand the cacophony this produces, I ordinarily shut off all forms of noise. This I did, brought the Pete up to about 35 mph at 2100 rpm and tried to get a feel for the road. Visibility wasn't a problem, but the road hadn't been ploughed recently. The passage of prior vehicles had produced ruts that approximated the lanes of travel, but made a firm grip on the wheel a necessity and led to randomly alternating patches of snow and ice. The grogginess quickly dispersed as I concentrated on keeping out of trouble.

I noticed as I backed off on the throttle approaching curves that the trailer was "pushing." This is caused by the desire of the trailer and its load to continue in a straight line while the tractor deviates to the left or right. It's nothing unusual. What was unusual was the strength of the push. Jeff was still awake. I said, "I thought this load was 28,000 lbs." "So did I," he said, fishing around for the piece of paper Emile gave us, "but it pushes more like 50,000." He found the piece of paper. "I guess that's why it feels like 50; this says it's 58." Okay, no problem. I'll adjust. Instead of backing off as I enter a curve, I'll back off before it, keep the power on through the curve, and that way I'll pull the trailer through rather than have it push me through. If I have to brake, I'll apply the trailer brakes first (there's a hand operated lever for the trailer brakes attached to the steering column) that way the trailer won't come around to kiss me.

Jeff got into the sleeper.

Traction isn't a problem. I focus on maintaining a steady speed around 35; keeping the rpms between 1800 and 2100; shifting smoothly; no sudden movements; a light touch on the braking lever; everything in slow motion, anticipating anything that might happen 500 to 1000 feet in front of me; and watching the rear views for anything that might happen behind me. Nothing happens. A car passes after following for miles in the enormous cone of old and new snow thrown up by the tires and propelled by the turbulent wash of air around the rig. Why did he wait so long?

Nothing happens. Jeff is asleep. If he's dreaming, I hope he's not dreaming about Emile. Rpms dropping off, pull the button over to high range, back off on the throttle, shift down, back on the throttle; rpms up, speed steady, curve coming up; ease back to 32, entering curve, back on the throttle, speed up to 36, button back to low, rpm at 2150; off the throttle, shift up, back on throttle; rpm 2000, speed 35, etc. etc. etc. The engine whines its mantra. I listen and time my movements to the chant. Nothing happens for hours. The snow's rate slackens as the sky lightens. I can see clouds. Pavement becomes visible, black-wet gaps in the white. I hear movement behind me. Jeff's awake.

"How we doin'?"

"We're doing. No problem."

"Where are we?"

"Almost in New York." [Jeff takes the shotgun seat, rubs his eyes and turns on the CB.]

"Road isn't bad."

"Getting better all the time."

"You tired?"

"Is a snake's ass close to the ground?"

"Pull into a rest area. I'll take over."

As we pull into a New York rest area, the CB is blatting news of a DOT check-point several miles ahead. We shut down the Pete and listen. We decide to get a little exercise and wait it out, hoping that in the interim, they'll move the checkpoint elsewhere. "Jeff," I say, "we don't have the bills for this load. We don't have the registration for this trailer either. Not only that, we don't have a signed trip lease and I think we're overweight on the rear axles. We might have a long wait." "Jessuz chrise, I don't need this shit," says Jeff. Exercise is good. We get coffee, wander around. The sun is trying to get by the clouds. It's approaching noon. Jeff says, "Screw it, let's go." We get in the truck.

As we pull out of the rest area, the CB is spreading the news that the DOT has moved and is heading toward the rest area. I look into the rear views and see a string of official vehicles slinking off the road into the rest stop lane. Another sign from god - maybe "resume safe speed."

We cross the Connecticut line, through Danbury, winding along 84 through gray hills, past Waterbury, then Farmington into the hell hole of Hartford and into Manchester. Jeff suggests that we stop in Vernon; get something to eat. We can stop at Abdow's. It has a parking lot big enough for the rig and we can call the girls (Roberta and Darlene) and they can join us. I say to Jeff: "Okay. But let me tell you how this conversation will go. She'll say, 'Where are you? Where have you been? You're late.'" "Whatever" says Jeff, "I think they'll be happy to hear from us." Right.

We stop at the K Mart Plaza in Vernon and go into Abdow's Big Boy. Jeff goes to the john; I go to the phone.

Ring - ring - ring.

"Hello?"

"Hi."

"Where are you?"

"Abdow's in Vernon. "

"Where have you been?"

"Oh, Pennsylvania, New York ..."

"We've been waiting. How come you're so late? "

"Yeah, I know, it's a long story. Why don't you and Dolly come down here and I'll tell you about it?"

"You know, you could have called. What have you been doing?"

"Not really. I'll explain when you get here. I'm pretty hungry. I'd like to get something to eat. Okay?"

"Okay. We'll be there in a few minutes."

Clunk

When Jeff joined me at a table I told him that the girls were on their way.

"Yeah, what'd they say?"

"Pretty much what I predicted."

"Dolly?"

"Mom."

"Jeez, why do they do that?"

"I don't know. I like to think that they worry, but they don't want to say that, so they act pissy instead. But that's only what I like to think. For all I know, they're slaves to hormonal pissiness. I never met a woman I could figure out."

"But you've known Mom all your life."

"Yeah. And she's been a mystery to me all my life. Maybe that's part of the attraction, ya' know: smart, beautiful and mysterious.

"Yeah, maybe. And Dolly's just like her."

"Whoa. Better stop talking. I think they just pulled in."

Indeed they had. They walked in, obviously mother and daughter; both beautiful; both with the same shade of bemused, skeptical "I just can't wait to hear the excuses" look on their faces. Roberta said that she had called my office to tell them that she had no idea of my whereabouts or my estimated time or day of arrival. I thanked her for that. We gave them a much abbreviated explanation of the last 18 hours of our lives. They seemed to buy our story. I couldn't fault them if they found some of it fairly bizarre.

There isn't much more to tell; the rest is rather anti-climactic. We ate, drank some coffee, said goodbye, got back into the truck, drove the 30 or so miles to Sturbridge, Mass., dropped off the trailer at its month old destination; and returned home.

As Jeff and I reviewed the experience, still vividly fresh, it had already taken on some attributes of comedy. In fact, I had seen some when Jeff first imitated Emile. And I meant what I said to Jeff. Life is either an adventure or an ordeal depending on how you see it. But it seems that you can't have an adventure without some measure of ordeal, and that the final characterization of the experience falls on one side or the other in accordance with its favorable or unfavorable outcome. Maybe it isn't an "either - or;" maybe it's an "and - both."

What do I know. I'll count this one as an adventure.

Anyway, that's the story. Curious, telling it seems to be just telling a story, something fabricated. But I'm really not that creative. Do you think I would (or could) make this stuff up just so I could write you a letter?

My love to you and Aunt Virginia.

Ed's Letter

Dear Uncle Fred,

I don't recall whether I have mentioned to you a guy named Ed. He and his spouse Susan are dear friends of ours and have been for about 25 years. Ed and I worked together for a few years a long time ago, but we stay in touch; visiting each other on an irregular basis, with the exception of spending two weeks together, virtually joined at the hip, during our tour of Ireland a year or so ago; an experience I thoroughly enjoyed - both the country and the company.

Ed is an intelligent, well-educated, well-read, well-rounded man, as comfortable wielding a hammer or paintbrush as a pen. One of his more endearing characteristics is his ability to recognize bullshit when he sees it and to employ his intellect and mastery of the language to expose the dung for what it is. Because he has a passion for the written word, I suggested that he read a few of the letters I have sent to you. This he did with probably the same reaction to those documents that you have had (a mixture of irritation and bemusement).

Anyway, I recently received a rather hefty envelope that bore the return address of my friend. Inside was a handwritten note that said:

Ron,

Turn about being fair play, and in view of my having suffered through your cathartic epistles to some mythical "Uncle Fred," I think you should be

subjected to my letter to the Hon. Sam Gjedenson, in response to one of those idiotic "surveys" one is always finding on one's doorstep. Please keep this - Susan thinks I'll be arrested, and may need a good lawyer!

Best, Ed

Attached was a letter to [U.S. Representative] Sam Gjedenson; a democrat for whom I did not vote in the last election, primarily because he has been in D.C. too long and now suffers from the "I'm a powerful guy - I know what's good for my constituents" syndrome. For your edification, elucidation and entertainment, I will now present the letter in its entirety. Ed, like you, has not seen fit to come into the 20th century. He has no computer, and the original letter is, thus, in longhand. It is typed here to save what's left of your eyesight.

"Subject: Attached Questionnaire

[Dear ....]

As a rule any such questionnaires which I receive are committed to the trash - their narrowly constructed "yes' or "no " answers seem to me a complete waste of time, paper and postage. On this occasion, however, I've decided to reply, the purpose of this letter being to qualify and elaborate upon my answers.
I will address each question in the order presented.

Question 1.   [Are you in favor of tougher penalties for 'those who commit crimes with firearms?] (Answer: "No")

In my opinion, the involvement of a firearm in any crime is absolutely irrelevant, and that the inclusion of a "firearm clause" in any criminal code is merely going to provide defense attorneys with more opportunity for technical hair-splitting; e.g., was the "firearm" loaded? Was it in operable condition? Was it pointed at the victim, or merely displayed or brandished?
My point is that all of our states' penal codes already deal with armed robbery, armed assault, assault with a deadly weapon, etc., and it seems to me that the general language of the underlying laws is quite appropriate and sufficient. Why should it matter whether the weapon was a shotgun, a knife, a crossbow, or a Louiseville Slugger? The essential elements are the same - someone has been placed in fear for his or her own life, and thereby relieved unlawfully of his or her property. To single out a particular weapon in applying our existing laws seems to me a meaningless, asinine consideration. Just toughen/enforce existing laws!

118

It is my belief that this whole issue of firearms is the most blatantly scarlet herring ever waved before the American public. To my mind, it represents just another band-aid hastily applied to conceal a festering social sore. (I will address this point in greater detail in my comments to Question 5.)

Question 2.   [Do you feel crime in your neighborhood has increased?] (Answer: "No")

I must describe this question as senseless. How does one "feel" an increase in crime? Is crime akin to temperature or humidity? I'm sure that comparative crime statistics are available to you for Middlesex County, Connecticut [where Ed & Sue live] so why don't you review them and tell me how I should "feel"! Shame on you!

[Question 3.   asked whether gangs were a problem in Ed's area. He answered "No" and left it at that]

Question 4.   [Do you believe we should put equal emphasis on prevention and punishment?] (Answer "Yes")

I answered "yes," but I'm really not qualified to answer such a question. "Prevention" of crime is much too broad an issue to address in trying to formulate a bill which can be expected to have any meaningful effect on crime in the immediate future. "Prevention" can range through welfare reform, hot school lunches, birth control education, economic recovery, school segregation, racial intolerance, ad infinitum. In short, if we try to deal with the general concept of "prevention" as part of an anti-crime bill, the end of the century will find us in worse shape than we are now.

There is no question, however, as to the importance of prevention, but let's try to put a workable handle on it for the purpose of an anti-crime bill. In other words, what realistic steps can be taken right now in the "area of prevention"?

A profoundly simple idea presents itself: how about if we simply avoid the morass of all the social, political, and moral issues embodied in the full concept of prevention and get down to the easily-understood principle of economics?

If I may be permitted an historical digression, let me take you back to New York in the 1880's and 1890's. Crime was a problem there [or 'then,' I can't decide which]. Gangs of "toughs" roamed the streets of the "tenderloin district" - - the "Dead Rabbits," the "Plug Uglies," the Monk Eastman Gang, to name a few. Forays into the more civilized sections of the city would occur from time to time, and when the citizenry became sufficiently outraged, "Something Was Done." Felonious and incompetent cops were dismissed, and a force of new, "clean," cops were able to pretty much eliminate the gangs.

119

What made this so easy? Because these primitive hoodlums had no economic base, they subsisted, for the most part, on stick-ups, petty thievery, strong-arm stuff, etc. But then, in 1918 came the Great Social Experiment known as Prohibition, which provided the New Underworld with a steady flow of cash which formed a solid financial base for future illegal activities.

O.K., so the Al Capones, the Bugsy Siegals, and (more recently) the John Gottis are now history, but in the meantime, a new financial opportunity for the underworld has been realized; one which makes the Prohibition "take" insignificant by comparison. I refer, of course, to the international drug trade. No one, I'm sure, can accurately estimate the amount of money generated by the drug trade.

Let us return to the streets of our present-day cities. How are the modern criminals able to buy these sophisticated "assault" weapons? How can 16-year olds be riding around in BMWs? Where is all the cash coming from? In view of my earlier dissertation, I think the answer is pretty obvious.

So, if we are willing to view "prevention" in realistic, short-term terms, why don't we make the slogan "the war against drugs" something more than that, thereby depriving the criminals of their principal source of income as well as their impetus for internecine violence? Let's deal with the economics of crime, and let the social services, the churches, etc., work on the other myriad avenues of "prevention."

We know where the plants from which cocaine, heroin, etc. are derived are growing. There is not a spot on the planet not visible, in minute detail, from devices already in orbit above the earth. We have the technological ability, moreover, to obliterate such sites, probably before I can finish this letter! A couple of superficial arguments could and have been made against such actions; i.e., the economic devastation of another country. Well, old Harry Truman did a pretty good job of devastating Japan's economy back in '45 and they recovered! That was war, one says - - is the "war against drugs/crime" a war, or just a bullshit slogan?

Another trite objection to such action would be the international reaction - - we are now the one and only super-power, so I guess we are in a position to do just about anything we view as morally and legally proper. Just for example, suppose we were to reduce Columbia to something resembling the Sahara Desert. The survivors would, in time, and with a little financial aid from us, find something to do. And to whom would we be answerable? After all, we would have been acting to eliminate a threat to our nation's survival, etc. Do we fear sanctions from Switzerland, or punitive action from Paraguay? In barracks parlance, would we really give a shit what the rest of the screwed-up world had to say?

My suggestion, therefore, would be the framing of an anti-crime bill which would focus on (a) stiffer penalties, strictly enforced, and (b) elimination by the most drastic means at our disposal of drug traffic in America. Try it. It will work. (The chief opposers, of course, will be those officials and law enforcers, great and small, who are deriving considerable unreported income from the drug trade.)

{A bibliographical note: Please find time to read Vincent Bugliosi's book "Drugs and America: the Case for Victory." "Seize the Moment" by Richard Nixon, is also a "must."}

Question 5. [Do you support a ban on assault weapons?] (Answer "No")

My problem with this question lies in the intrinsically vague nature of the term "assault weapon." As Rush Limbaugh pointed out in one of his books "... words [are supposed to] mean something." When I went to school, the word "assault" could be used as either a verb, or as a noun, never as an adjective. It would seem, however, that the Orwellian "Newspeak " of Washington has decided to employ "assault" as an adjective. Let's consider this: I have a little knife in my kitchen, with which I normally peel vegetables. It has a 2" blade, but it is quite sharp. I suppose that if I were to use it to slit someone's throat, it would thereby become an "assault" knife, whereas it had previously been a "paring," "peeling," or "slicing" knife. Do you follow me? (The possible examples are endless.)

So now we have a laboriously constructed list of some 18 or 19 "assault weapons" which should be banned, to be presented to a President [Clinton] who wouldn't know the difference between an M-16 and a Daisy Red Ryder BB gun. (I loved the dialogue about bayonet studs -- how many drive-by shootings, do you suppose, are done with fixed bayonets?!!) Shouldn't the Congress and Senate be reminded that under federal law ownership by private citizens of automatic weapons is already banned? I can't go out and buy a Goddammed machine gun - besides, I doubt that I could afford one, since I'm not a drug dealer!

In retrospect, I'm not sure why I wrote this very long letter. I'm sufficiently cynical to know that you'll never read it. I'll get an acknowledgment (a form letter) from one of your Candy Stripers - you'll get a very brief resume about [a letter] from some nut from Middletown, and I'll continue to find your sophomoric questionnaires in my mailbox.

Sic transit gloria mundi,[22]

[signed]

P.S.

You should be aware of the fact that the views I've expressed are shared by quite a few of my Connecticut contemporaries. Most of us (heretofore the

---

[22] So passes away the glory of the world.

"silent majority") are getting a bit tired of non-representative, prostituted "representation." You are in a position to do something which might earn you a place in American history - - why not go for it - - you'll be dead for a long time! We all will!"

Well, ya know somethin'? Reading Ed's letter again reminds me of somebody else. Doesn't it? Yeah, it does. Come on; you could have written it.

For that matter, I could have too. About a year ago, I replied, at length of course, to a mindless survey sent to me by another politician who allegedly represents me. In my reply to what questions were presented, and what questions should have been presented, I gave my alleged representative a brief, but accurate, lesson in basic economics and finance, something about which neither she nor her staff apparently have a clue. I did not receive an acknowledgement of any sort. I wasn't surprised. I wonder why dear old Sam G didn't send me a questionnaire?

You've probably heard by now that Lynn (remember, my sister, the Patra?[23]) managed somehow to acquire two tickets to see (and hear) Pavarotti when he plays the Foxwood Casino. This is big-time stuff. Lynn got the tickets for my mother (you know her, your sister Claire - la Giapponese[24]) and Uncle Godfrey (your brother) who is going with my mother (i.e., your sister). Lynn (i.e., my sister, but your niece) will drive them to the Casino, where they will be the guests of the Mashantucket Pequot Indians (not relatives - to the best of my knowledge). Uncle Gog will stay a few days, and it is my intention to annoy him for a while during his sojourn.

We've haven't talked in a while. I will call you after Uncle Gog's visit, unless something noteworthy occurs in the meantime. I assume you follow the same guideline that I do; namely, no news is good news.

Try to stay well and out of trouble. Give our love to Aunt Virginia.

---

[23] Short for Cleopatra. Nicknamed by Uncles Fred and Godfrey because she was treated as a little queen.
[24] "Japanese." Nicknamed by her mother, Carmela, because of the shape of her eyes.

122

The Lunkhead Syndrome

Dear Uncle Fred,

I hope that this letter finds you in your normal state of good humor, excellent health and happy-go-lucky perspective. Uh-huh.

Even if you're not in that kind of mood, I intend by way of the following commentary to get you to lighten-up a bit. I have no fixed topic in mind, and I will no doubt ramble in a seemingly unguided misuse of a good number of pieces of paper. I thought I'd start off with some observations that relate, sort of, to my last letter wherein (if I may direct your flagging memory) I told you that I opted for a career in the corporate law arena.

Being an employee of a large corporation is not suitable for everyone. Being a lawyer working for a large corporation is suitable for relatively few. Being a corporate lawyer in the corporate law department of a large corporation is suitable for even fewer. I was in the last category (you can interpret that in either a positive or negative manner, whichever you think applies). The corporation I worked for is a large financial services "institution." One of the things it sells is insurance (life insurance, auto, homeowners, annuities, etc). I think it is only a mild overstatement to say that it is difficult to make money by selling insurance.

Nobody really wants it. Nobody likes it. Nobody wants to pay for it. Most people have it only because they need (or think they need) it. It is fair to note that insurance salesmen are held in less esteem than car salesmen (although, in candor, my information is that lawyers rank well below both in the common man's hierarchy of admiration). This is as it should be. People buy insurance, of whatever type, because they are afraid. They are afraid that they might get hurt, become ill, T-bone a busload of grandmas with their car, have some bozo slip on the sidewalk, burn the house down, have a flood, not live long enough or live too long, etc., etc. Preying on peoples' fears to sell them something they don't want is a questionable business.

Making money doing that is, in common sentiment, immoral. The low esteem in which such companies are regarded is largely responsible for the governmental oversight focused on them. Their business practices in general and insurance rates, in particular, are regulated by every state, and the federal government is seeking to impose national standards.

Don't get me wrong, I think that there is nothing immoral about making money (as long as it's done through legal means). Seeking profit from one's efforts is what made this country great. But the reality is that there is scant little margin for profit in the rates that companies are allowed to charge for insurance. My point is that that is not where the money is to be made anyway.

So, you think I'm nuts. Why do these companies exist if they can't manage to skim off a few bucks from the premium they get? Good question. In part, they make money on the money they're holding to pay claims. In other words, cash passes through their hands. While it is in their hands, they invest it and the money earned by investment stays with them. More significantly, they also provide investment services for billions of dollars of retirement plan monies. Like a mutual fund, they charge fees for their services and that is the source of much of their income. Because "insurance" companies act like banks and mutual funds they're called financial services companies.

Now, why have I bored you with this? Because, the point is that in terms of profit margins, we're not talking about percentage points, we're usually talking about "basis" points (i.e., tenths of a percent). Two things should be immediately apparent, even to a person like you who is being forced to read this dull drivel and is slowly losing consciousness. First, unless there is money coming in the door, there is no hope of making any profit. And, second, unless expenses are kept to an absolute minimum, there is no hope of making any profit.

Selling stuff was never my forte. I have no interest in being a salesman of any sort. I know next to nothing about insurance; I don't know why your homeowner's coverage costs so much, or why it excludes hail damage. I do know enough about the uses of money, however, to maintain only a minimal amount of life insurance. Why should I provide an unmerited reward to my ungrateful heirs? Besides, when I croak, I want it to be a sad day for everybody.

My job had nothing to do with insurance, it (in part) was to help the "business people" make business deals that would make money. Another part of my job was to prevent situations from arising which might motivate employees (and former employees) to sue the company, and if they did sue, to prevent them from winning. In other words, much of my focus was on the "expense" side of the profit coin. Any small businessman will tell you that getting a dollar in the door is a good thing, but if your expenses eat up too much of that dollar, you're on the road to Chapter XI or worse. Small businessmen live or die by watching every penny of expense and making sure that they're not expending any funds in an unnecessary or non-productive manner.

But in a large corporation, even a financial services corporation, it seems these simple guides to healthy profits somehow become lost or ignored. Let me give you a couple of examples to demonstrate the point.

One of my early childhood memories is the V - man calling a guy named Guido "Lunkhead." I don't claim to have understood what that meant at the time I first heard it; only that it caught my attention because it had the ring of disrespect. As I became aware of the interplay of personalities and the distinctions between the behaviors of adult individuals, I recognized that Guido was a loud-mouth. He was able to pontificate on any subject and had a complete mastery of the obvious. On complex matters he could reach momentous, and often erroneous, conclusions without any discussion (let alone demonstration) of the facts I guess that's why my father called him Lunkhead.

As you have probably noticed, there are more horses' asses (i.e., lunkheads) in the world than there are horses. Many of the excess of the former over the latter are at large in the business world, and I think I've managed to come into contact with more than my share. For example, a number of years ago a big envelope marked "Personal & Confidential - to be Opened by Addressee Only" arrived on my desk. It had (of course) already been opened by my lovely and talented secretary (Donna), who threw it in front of me, saying,

"You're going to love this."

I was neither surprised nor concerned that Donna had opened the envelope. She was under instructions to do so. Experience has shown that such an envelope cannot be "personal" because if it were "personal" it would not have been delivered through the normal inter-office mail bearing a printed address label. Nor could it be "confidential" because a packet that large would have involved many people in its preparation, thus assuring that whatever it contained was no secret, but rather its substance had been communicated (because it was labeled confidential) in one distorted form or another throughout the employee population by way of the rumor mill.

No - materials that are truly personal or confidential are communicated by hand delivery, by the U.S. Mail, or by electronic mail (usually sent during the dead of night). The fact that it said "to be Opened by Addressee Only" was disregarded because Donna is of Italian ancestry and, as such, wouldn't divulge a confidence if bamboo splinters were driven under her fingernails. While I'm at it, I should tell you that Donna has the classic face of Italian women you've seen in Renaissance paintings. However, I would quickly add that her "attitude" is of the Lady MacBeth variety: "look like the innocent flower, but be the serpent under it." Anyway, I tossed the package aside.

When I got around to it a few days later, I found that it was from one of those departments that seem to pop-up only in those corporations which have the luxury of extra office space and a loose hand on the corporate till. It was from a person I had never heard of who had an impressive title (one connoting a six figure salary) and represented a department called "Strategic Development and Oversight"(SD&O) or some such important-sounding euphemism for a money sucking, non-productive unit.

The cover memo said I had been selected to join an elite group (of about 200 people), to "provide [my] valuable counsel and keen insights" by answering some 18 questions (with multiple sub-part questions) so that, upon tabulation and aggregation of the responses, the SD&O Department could furnish senior management with an "action blueprint" (as opposed, I presume, to a regulation blueprint, or perchance a "plan") which would " ... assess the impact of evolving trends and define the parameters of the strategic factors which will drive the vision of the Company in the coming decade."

You'll observe that the language is not intended to foster clarity. Indeed, since the pen is the mirror of the mind, clarity of communication is well nigh impossible because that would presuppose clarity of thought. The use of empty words is a screen for the fact that they are incapable of meaningful, let alone clear, thought. The pomposity of the verbiage is an attempt to mystify the audience into believing that some process of profound ratiocination has taken place, and that we are to take these words seriously.

You should also recognize that these people wouldn't know a strategy from a tactic if one bit them in the ass. Virtually any awareness of a possible future event and a plan to handle the possibility is termed a strategy. In your frame of reference, this is like saying that your plan to kill the guys who were trying to kill you wasn't a tactic; it was a strategy.[25] This misconception further muddles the process because while they talk strategy what they do is plan for short-term, short-lived, immediate objectives (like making this quarter's financial results look good, even at the expense of long-term profit).

At the time this questionnaire was devised, senior management was persuaded (because it was all the rage at other companies) that the company needed a "mission statement" (I suppose something like Bull Halsey's[26] admonition to "kill more Japs") and that it needed to "formulate strategies" and "re-engineer," "reinvent" and "redefine" the business. Recognize these bubble headed buzzwords? You should. Slick Willy and his arrogant airhead cronies use them.

Disregard the seemingly grandiose connotations of the words and the fact that such overly broad generalizations can mean anything one might want them to mean. What the words mask is the reality that the business was not doing well; management hadn't the foggiest idea why or how to make it do better; and the appearance of doing something - anything - would be better than doing nothing. As the V-man says, a coat of paint will hide a multitude of sins.

In aid of the appearance of "addressing the critical issues" and "positioning the Company to seize the initiative through innovative implementation of

---

[25] Uncle Fred was a WWII Pacific combat vet. He fought on little island hell-holes that don't even appear on your maps of the world. He survived some horrific battles, but was nearly killed by malaria and denge fever.
[26] Admiral William F. Halsey, WW II Pacific Fleet.

our vision," there emerged a host of "consultants," "analysts," "facilitators" and other parasitic, energetic, self-aggrandizing, "experts" whose primary function is to fortify management's egocentric delusion that it can create a new reality by proclamation. They do this by taking surveys, conducting "studies," producing charts and graphs (in color), holding meetings, preparing "option papers," circulating memos and articles by like minded experts, devising "decision trees" (or "landscapes"), and otherwise creating fabric for the emperor's new clothes. I don't fault these consultants/opportunists for taking advantage of fuzzy-thought management; that would be like blaming the flies for the dung heap.

All this would be mildly amusing but for the fact that it is taken very seriously and it costs a tremendous amount of time and, therefore, money. The result is that, through this process of institutionalized obsequiousness, even the most hair-brained, wrong-headed, counter-productive, "new and innovative" (mis)conception can take on a life of its own and play out as if it had some foundation in reality; wasting time and diverting attention from the only justification for a corporation's existence - making money for its shareholders.

The survey I started to tell you about (a few pages back) was a piece of one of these unguided efforts.

The purpose of the survey was to "identify emerging trends" in and "structure strategies with respect to" the "critical human resources issues" which would "position" the company to be "highly responsive" to the "intensely competitive environment of the future." There were several things (in addition to the fatuous jargon) that immediately annoyed me. First, the questions were phrased in a way which presumed that we were not then in an "intensely competitive environment" which, of course, we had been for decades, and that whatever had been done to this point was "wrong" (forgetting the fact that under earlier, less ponderous, less self-deluded, management the company had been quite successful - its stock price being in the middle $60s when the Dow was around 2800, whereas its current price is about $56 with the Dow around 3800).

But specifically, for example, the first series of questions sought, by limiting responses to a fixed number of possible answers in each case, to "identify" the seven "primary" human resources issues of the decade. Why do you suppose they picked seven; symmetry with the seven deadly sins or the seven cardinal virtues; seven days of the week; seven come eleven? The possible answers ranged from compensation and benefits to "workforce diversity" with a bunch of other items like skills, productivity, flexible hours and "alternative work schedules," technology "impact," legislation, education and a bunch of other stuff.

Well, just how the hell is anyone supposed to go about ranking such factors? Why am I limited to seven factors? Who gives a rat's ass about "diversity" whatever that's supposed to mean? Why was I annoyed? Because I knew that, whatever my answers might be, they would be tabulated along with all the other answers without any thought, let alone recognition, of the reality that all the "factors" are interrelated, interdependent, and are pieces of an inseparable whole. In other words, for example, how could I say that attracting the most highly qualified employees is a primary factor without attaching to it those other factors which would, in fact, attract such people; e.g., competitive-plus compensation and benefits, progressive management, opportunities for advancement, friendly environment, long term financial stability of the company, etc.? Of what possible use is "diversity" if to achieve that diversity you hire people who don't have the necessary skills (e.g., the ability to think, to read, to speak English)? Oh, you think I exaggerate? Explain this:

"Hi, Ron, this is Shirley in Human Resources? [formerly called "personnel"] I think I've got a problem."

"Well, you just tell uncle Ron what it is and we'll see what we can do."

"Well, … ya know, we run sort of a second shift that calls policyholders and they, like, … ya know … ask them questions about service and stuff?"

"Uh-huh"

"Well, like, they hired this guy last week and it turns out that, he's … like …deaf. "

"Is he 'like' deaf, or is he in fact deaf?"

"No, he's really deaf."

"You must be shitting me."

"Nu-uh. He says he's deaf."

"Well, what the hell do you want me to do? Tell him he doesn't have a job. Send him packing."

"But, can we do that?"

"Of course you can do that. Why are you asking me that question?"

"Because, … like, ya know, … he's … ya know, ... handicapped."

"Yeah. He can't hear. So?"

"So, we can't fire him because we can't discriminate against people who have handicaps, right?"

"Wrong. Sufferin' christ, woman, the law says we can't unfairly discriminate against people with handicaps. It doesn't say that we have to let a deaf guy do telephone work. This guy doesn't have the ability to do the job. He is unable to hear, he is without the capacity for listening, he does not function in the auditory environment, his ears are shut and stopped, he is like a doorknob, a doornail or a post. The man is deef! Would you force the electric company to hire quadriplegic linesmen?"

"Well, don't they have to make 'reasonable accommodations'?"

"Like what? Have him splice wires with his teeth? The point is that this guy can't do the job. Period. We're not running a charitable institution, a halfway house, it's a business. How the hell did he get hired in the first place? Didn't he fill out an employment application?"

"Well, … yeah … I guess so."

"What do you mean you guess so? Everybody has to fill out an application."

"What's the big deal about ... ya know ... the application? Like ... what difference does it make?"

"The difference, my little 'human resources professional' is that there is a statement on that form which asks whether there is any reason the applicant would be prevented from performing the duties of the job for which he is applying. If he didn't put down that he was deaf - or hard of hearing - then he lied on his application. That form also says that lying on the form constitutes grounds for immediate termination of employment."

"Oh, is that right? ... It says that?"

"Yes, it does. I strongly suggest that you read it. I know I'm going to read yours."

It was incidents like this which led me to observe during one of those god-awful, expense containment meetings, that if we wanted to save some money what we should do is line up all the employees (some 48,000 at that point) and shoot every third one, thus reducing most expenses by one third with no decrease, and perhaps an increase, in productivity. No one laughed. Cripes, did they think I was serious? Were they mulling it over?

In any event, I found it impossible to answer the survey questions in any meaningful way. I mean that literally. The answers would have had no meaning because the questions were meaningless. No matter what tabulation, synthesis, chart or graphic were produced, it would not embody facts upon which a strategy (or even a tactic) could be soundly based. So I sent a memo to SD&O that said something like this:

"I am flattered that you have asked me to participate in the survey. I am, however, constrained to advise you that I have returned the questionnaire in the same pristine condition that it arrived. It is not without some trepidation that I do this. Let me explain.

I think you would agree that only facts are reasons for action. The questions posed, and the choice of answers to each question are so abstracted (removed) from facts that both question and answer can achieve no more than a generalization about issues which are, factually, extremely complex, interrelated and interdependent. Justice Holmes said that, " A generalization is empty so far as it is general." And a general "proposition isn't worth a damn." I agree with Holmes.

Each question and each choice of answer is expressive of a conclusion (in the form of an opinion) that is grounded, not on facts, but on little more than a guess about two things. One, what the current facts are and, two, what the facts might be in the future. I could give you my generalized response to your generalized questions, but that would be one guess imposed on another. I think you would be poorly served to use my guess as a basis on which to propose any strategy to senior management; sort of like trying to make a silk purse of a sow's ear.

If you want my counsel and insight, it is this: withdraw the questionnaire. Of course, this is only one man's opinion and you should feel free to do whatever you think prudent."

Well, you would think that I had penned an obscene parody of the company's theme song. There was an almost immediate and clearly hostile reaction to my comments and, more particularly, my advice. Of course, this response to my guided missal was not directed to me, but to its addressee's immediate superior who, shocked at the inhuman treatment suffered by his subordinate, did not take the matter up with me, but went to his superior, who went to his superior, until the unfortunate affair reached one of the three most senior of the senior management team. My first notice of the flap came from the secretary of said senior member, who called and said:

"You are such an asshole."

"Thank you for noticing. What's going on now?"

"Well, smart guy, it seems that you have somehow skewered someone's sacred cow."

"I love alliteration. Tell me more."

"Okay, try this: look, love, little letters can leave large lacerations in limp egos. Get my drift? I think you'll be hearing from our semi-illustrious boss."

"Not bad. I get your drift. Is he pissed, or what?"

"I think you'll find out. Act surprised."

This conversation illustrates one of the few generalizations that I have found valid: it is more important to get along with the boss's secretary than to get along with the boss. Two days later, I was in the big boys' bailiwick, leaving a meeting, when the senior aforementioned confronted me.

"Hey, Ron, come in here for a minute. Sit down. [I did as instructed] Want a coffee?"

"No thanks."

"Tell me something. Why are you compelled to be such an asshole?"

"I don't think it's a compulsion. It's something I've worked for years to perfect."

"Well, you're good at it, I'll grant you that. Listen, I heard about your memo on that survey thing. You got a lot of people upset."

"So I've heard. That wasn't my intention, My Benevolence."

"Yeah, well, the road to hell is paved with good intentions. Don't misunderstand me; we've always talked man to man, so I'll tell you up front that I don't give a flying duck that these people are upset, and I care even less about the dip-shit survey. [At this point I was wishing that I had a tape recorder]. You know as well as I that this place - hell, the whole world - runs because it's liberally greased with bullshit. By writing that memo you interrupted the bullshit brigade."

"I was only telling it like I see it."

"That's not the problem, Ron. The problem is you told the wrong people. Nobody wants to hear that they're devoting their energy to troweling out bullshit. It hurts their feelings. Besides, every once in a while these assholes stumble on an honest-to-god idea."

"*Etiam porcinus caecus glantem aliquando invenit*, eh?"

"What?"

"Even a blind pig occasionally finds an acorn."

"Jesus christ! That's what I'm talking about, you smart-ass! You give some people the impression that you're a snotty intellectual; you tell them they can't make chicken soup out of chicken shit; and they resent it. They resent you."

"I don't give a shit; and that's not what I said."

"What *didn't* you say?"

"You can't make chicken soup out of chicken shit."

"It wasn't? What *did* you say?"

"I said you can't make a silk purse of a sow's ear."

"Jesus christ! Same thing."

"No, My Liege, it isn't."

"Yeah it is!"

"I still don't give a shit."

"Neither do I, but I don't need the aggravation. Next time you feel like telling it like it is, whisper it in my ear. Jezzuz-god! I don't need this! I'm trying to run a company here! Speaking of which - get out."

Now, you should have noticed that this silly topic had taken up the time of a host of very highly paid people, distracting them from productive tasks and irritating every one of them. You should also notice that even though the "senior" thought it was a waste of time, the project was not halted in its tracks and its originators banished to the unemployment line. *Au contraire, Zio.*[27] The lone dissenter had been silenced and the project went ahead with renewed vigor. In time (about six months) the "results" of the survey were disclosed to the management team. With great satisfaction and self congratulations all around the aggregated, tabulated, synthesized and sterilized responses were presented in recognition of the presumed intellectual level of the audience - in color coded pie-charts (which by now were deemed *de rigueur*). What the charts showed, as I interpreted them with the aid of their accompanying (sophomoric) commentary, was that it is indeed impossible to induce a meaningful response to a meaningless question.

Yep, by god, wages would be important; so would benefits, especially medical and pensions benefits; so would opportunities for advancement; ditto for technology and "diversity." Well, I guess we learned a lot. So, late at night, I sent an "E mail" to the senior that said:

---

[27] To the contrary, Uncle.

"M' Lord,

I assume you have seen the results of the quintessential survey. I was wrong. This great company has the action blueprint for its glorious emergence into the 21st century. Now I can return to my mundane labors knowing that there is a grand design and that all is right with the world."

The next morning I had a reply:

"Personal & Confidential Vassal,

1) I did see the results.

2) Kindly shut your yap."

So I shut my yap and went on with my work. One of the subjects of that work was a continuing saga that had developed after we had sold off a piece of one of our diversified operations to a group of employees who had been managing that piece. This was one of those (highly) leveraged buyouts you may have heard about during the '80s, and these former employees (now the owners) had, during the negotiations, sought to gain any financial advantage they could possibly imagine, at our expense. This is, of course, to be expected in any negotiation; when the target is far off, you aim high.

Unfortunately, some of their more overreaching negotiating points had been accepted by our sometimes less than astute business people, with the result that the new owners had it in their heads that if they asked for something, we'd give it to them.

But things had changed. Because the sale was completed, the business people who had been so generous in the past were no longer involved. They had moved on to other transactions - which would more than likely erode the corporate coffers - and had no interest in this matter. The "boys" (as I came to call them) now had to deal with me because whatever they thought the "deal" to be was contained in written documents that purportedly set out the entire agreement, including specified future liabilities arising out of the transaction. In other words, we had a contract. Contracts are "legal" things. I'm a lawyer. I get to say what the contract "means;" and the only person who can overrule me is a judge. I bet you're impressed, eh?

Anyway, we had had a running dispute about a number of things that they said the contract meant (each of which would have cost us money) and I had consistently deflected their assertions; not because I'm a bad guy and not because they would have cost us, but because they were just plain wrong. I could tell that they were becoming annoyed. Poor babies. They complained to the senior.

"Hey, A H [asshole] the boss wants you here ... now."

"I hear ya. I'll be there when I get there."

"No, no. Now."

I had a cigarette, went to the latrine, then went upstairs.

"Took you long enough to get here."

"I'm a busy man. I can't jump up every time you need something."

"Sit down and shut up. [I sat down] I've just had a call from Charlie. You've been handling the [XYZ Company] thing?"

"Yeah?"

"Well, Charlie says that you've been giving his boys a hard time about some picky little bullshit stuff."

"If you call a potential $20 million liability 'picky little bullshit stuff' that's right."

"Where do you get $20 million?"

"From my calculator. Amazing gadgets, ya know. You put numbers in, tell it to add, divide, multiply or whatever and magic - it gives you a number: $20 million, give or take a few."

"Don't give me shit, how did you come up with that number? He said it would be something like 10% of that."

"Either he's a damn fool or he's a liar, and since when is $2 mil 'little'?"

"Look, I don't want to argue about this. The point is that I'm being told you're a real hard-ass, for no reason."

"And you believe that?"

"Yeah, I believe that you're a hard-ass. That's why I pay you an outrageous salary. That's why I put up with your bullshit. I just want to be sure you're not being an unreasonable hard-ass; that you're being a hard-ass only when you should be; that you're not pissing people off without a good reason."

"Oh, yea of little faith, I have good reasons. These schmuks have been taking us for a ride, but it's over. The agreement isn't a model of clarity, but it can't possibly be construed the way they want it. No judge in his right mind would believe we could have been so stupid that we gave the boys some sort of equity participation in the profits of our insurance subsidiaries."

"What?"

"That's what the boys are claiming."

"That's gotta be wrong."

"Have I been talking to myself, here? Of course it's wrong."

"Okay. Okay. That can't be right. Do what you've gotta do. [waving his hand] Get out."

Two weeks later I received, by certified mail, a letter from the boys' attorneys politely informing me that unless I became more tractable, they would have no choice but to initiate litigation in their local, friendly, neighborhood, federal court. To make my task easier, and to indicate their serious intent, attached to this polite letter was a "courtesy copy" of the complaint that they would file.

I read the courtesy copy with interest and amusement. You should under-stand that it is the obligation of an attorney to tell his client's story (even if it's a fantasy) in its most plausible aspect. That is, in a way that will, with some luck, satisfy a judge that somewhere in that story there is a shred (a "scintilla" as we say) of a possibility, even if one must suspend disbelief, that some sort of valid dispute might be discerned. For practical legal purposes, "dispute" just means inconsistent claims with respect to the same subject matter, so it is no real feat to make it sound like there's a dispute. Of course, courts are in the business of settling disputes and each complaint is, there-fore, grist for the mill. Such things are also a boon to the lawyers because litigation is our business and we are loath to turn business away. Receiving complaints is business as usual and, as my friend Wayne says, "file it - when it comes in, I'll throw it on the pile with the rest of them."

In this instance, however, and despite the valiant efforts of counsel for the boys to - pick one - make a silk purse of a sow's ear, make chicken soup from chicken shit, clothe the emperor, find an acorn, the assertions made in the courtesy copy of the complaint were so contrived, so transparent, so bloody unbelievable, that even the most stupid, political hack, appointee to the bench would laugh it off the calendar. I suppose I could have taken it se-riously and responded to the inane assertions point by point. But that would be a waste of time and paper, so I called a guy I knew quite well who worked for the boys.

"Hi, Chuck, how the hell are ya?"

"Hey, Ron, how are things in gross Hard-up-ford, Connecticut?"

"Just ducky, as usual. What's with you?"

"SOS [same old shit]. I've been hearing your name taken in vain around here. Hee-hee, 'the boys' are all pissed-off 'cause you won't play fair. Ain't you got no sympathy?"

"If they're looking for sympathy, they'll find it in the dictionary right af-ter shit. Listen up, Chuckles, I want you to do me a favor."

"Oh, christ, I knew it, goddamn lawyers always want something."

"You don't have to say yes 'til you hear it. I would remind you, however, that you owe me one."

"Yeah, yeah, tell me what 'it' is, dickwad."

"Tell them that they can kiss my dago ass, I'll see them in court."

"Argh! Not a pretty picture! My god, have some mercy! I just ate! Hee-heehee, [cough - cough] come to think of it, I'd pay big bucks to see that. You really want me to say that?"

"Yeah, I'm perfectly serious."

"Let me get this straight. You want me to say - I'm writing this down - Ron says you can kiss his dago ass, he'll see you in court. How do you spell 'dago'?"

"Don't give me shit. You gonna do it, or no?"

"Yeah, I'll do it, with the greatest of pleasure. Ha-ha-hee." [cough-cough]

"You oughta back off on those Camels, Chuckles."

What I didn't know was that another copy of the courtesy complaint had been sent to a member of the Senior Management Team, but not the senior aforementioned. This was not a good thing. The S.M.T. member that received it (a big-man in the company) was not exactly a fan of mine. We had had a few differences of opinion in the recent past, one of which took place in front of the entire S.M.T. Big man opened the meeting something like this:

"I want to know why it is that every time I want to do something, he [me] says that I can't. The trouble with this company is that there are too many god damned lawyers and their shit ass rules."

You'll note that profanity is not uncommon at "high" management levels. This bit of anti-attorney profanity was common. So common, in fact, that Wayne and I had shortened it and used it ourselves as "GDLs and SARs."

"Every time I turn around there's a lawyer saying, 'no you can't do that.' Who's running this company anyway? I want him [me] to tell me why I can't do this."

"I'm not saying that you can't do what you want to do. In fact, it is rare that I give a flat-out 'no' opinion."

"Then, what the hell are you saying?"

"What I'm saying is that because no one outside this room knows of this proposal, an immediate implementation will come as a shock to all the employees, whether they are affected by it or not. Many will be upset and angry - because we're taking something away - and angry people sue. There is a significant risk that, in that event, we may not be able to successfully defend a suit at this point. And if we're not successful, we won't be able to implement at all. I'm suggesting that we make a low-keyed announcement through normal channels that a change will be made later on this year."

"What good will that do? Why wait?"

"By announcing now and implementing later, the relatively few people affected and angry will have the opportunity to vent. We'll know who they are and can handle them on an individual basis, if need be. The litigation risk will be dramatically reduced, maybe eliminated. We'll save a lot of money and get what you want done."

In this instance, it was my misfortune that an even bigger big-man of the company agreed with me. There followed a debate between the big-men in which no other member of the meeting dared participate. The bigger big-man prevailed, but there was no cause for glee, quite the contrary. In the corporate world, displeasure never flows up, it pours down. I was down stream. When big-man saw the complaint he was primed.

"What do you intend to do about this complaint? Gonna save me a zillion dollars are ya?"

"Nothing."

"Nothing? What do you mean nothing?"

"I mean I'm going to do nothing more than what I've already done."

"What have you already done; settled it for a mere half a zillion dollars?"

"No, I told the boys to kiss my dago ass."

"You did what?"

"Told them to kiss my dago ass."

"You can't do that!"

"I've already done it."

"But ... but ... you can't do that! Who the hell do you think you are?"

"I'm Counsel for the company against which the complaint would be filed if it is filed, which it won't. And even if it were, it wouldn't have a snowball's chance in hell of getting past a motion to dismiss."

"You've got a goddamn cavalier attitude! This could be a big problem! How the hell do you know it won't go to trial?"

"It's my job to know. That's why you pay me the big bucks."

"You arrogant little shit!"

"I believe, sir, that is *argumentem ad hominem* ..."[28]

"I don't know what that means, but you can believe this: this isn't over! Does [the senior aforementioned] know about this?

"Not yet."

[rattle - clunk]

Well, that was exhilarating. I love using the little Latin I know to piss people off. It always does. Why is that? It was about ten minutes later that I received another call.

"A.H.?" [the boss' secretary]

"Yeah?"

"My boss and yours, you know, His Severity?"

"Yeah."

"Well, he just had a visitor. This visitor apparently had an unpleasant experience with you recently."

"Yeah."

"Well, he was unpleasant with His Severity. Now His Severity is being unpleasant and wants to focus some, maybe all, of that on you. So would you kindly get your *dago ass* over here?"

"Yeah."

"See you soon." [sweetly]

When I got there, the senior was sitting behind his big desk with his face in his hands.

"Ronnie, Ronnie, Ronnie. What am I going to do about you? [the accused stood mute] Why did you tell [the boys] to kiss your ass?"

"Dago ass, My Exactitude."

"Oh, yes, of course. Your dago ass. But why?"

---

[28] An argument directed against a person's character rather than the facts; e.g., dismissing a person's statement because that person has an odd hairstyle.

"Because I had some sort of, apparently vain, expectation that I could eliminate a lot of wasted energy by letting them know in no uncertain terms that we weren't going to put up with their bullshit."

"But, surely, you could have done that in a more, shall we say, urbane manner."

"That method hasn't worked. I chose to use a guttural approach."

"You know who was just here?"

"Yes."

"You know he wants to use this against you?"

"Sure."

"And you don't care."

"Bingo."

"I can't defend you very well on this one. What do you intend to do?"

"If he's intent on making this a big deal, the only people he can make it a big deal with are the members of the board of directors. I'll get to them before he does. I'll tell one of the board members exactly what's going on and leave it to him, and them."

"I guess that's right. Do it. Get out."

So I called the board member I knew best and told him in detail the whole sordid story. There was a lengthy pause, then:

"... ah. Hee-hee. ... Ah-haw, haw, haw. Hee - hee - hee -ah- hah, hah, hah...god damn, shit almighty, that's delicious. I wish I were there to see their faces, those greedy bastards. Damn, Ron, that's marvelous, 'bout time somebody showed 'em some reality. Hey, don't worry about [big man] I'll take care of that. Thanks for calling, that's the funniest thing I've heard all week."

I reported to the senior aforementioned the disclosure and the response. He seemed relieved. The matter was never again discussed. The complaint was never filed. But that isn't the point.

The point is that virtually the entire affair was a waste of time, needlessly deflected the attention of people receiving extraordinary compensation from the duties for which they were being paid those enormous salaries, and infringed on the autonomy of the very people whose duty it is to make the decisions in the first place. If senior people spend some of their time on this silly shit, what other foolishness occupies the rest of their time? Does it come as a surprise that no one really thinks "globally," or "outside the box," or "strategically" (or whatever other flaming buzzword is the idiot idiom of the moment)? Would you let Guido run your business?

I didn't think so.

But enough. My blood pressure is rising.

By the way, (re our last telephone conversation) I thought you were issued 15 round mags for your M-1 carbine. Maybe in the old days, when you used yours (I assume you weren't carrying an '03 Springfield in the jungle) they were 10 rounds?[29] Also, I'm sure you'll be happy to know that those frig-gin Arisakas[30] that were firing in your direction in the '40s were still being used, and with similar intent, in the early '60s. Just thought I'd pass that on.

And, really, shooting at seagulls with a Ma Deuce?[31] Tsk, tsk, I guess boys will be boys whatever the circumstances.

Our love to you and Aunt Virginia.

---

[29] Uncle Fred liked the carbine because it is small and light; and you can carry more ammo. However, he preferred the M1 Garand because it has more "knock-down power." He said that sometimes a "Nip" hit with a carbine round would get up and come at him again. When they were hit by the Garand, they stayed down.

[30] Japanese 6.5mm, fixed magazine, bolt action, general issue rifle.

[31] 50 caliber machine gun, designated M2, and affectionately called Ma Deuce.

138

The Sayings of the V - man

Dear Uncle Fred,

I t was good to talk with you about my father.
Before starting this letter, I scanned the last letter I sent you just to remind myself of what that was about and avoid repeating myself. I became aware of the fact that many of the things I said in that letter were things my father said. I wasn't surprised. Not long ago I acknowledged to my father that I had said to Roberta, "I'm turning into my father. I not only look like him, I act like him, and I talk like him." He had a quizzical look on his face, so I quickly added that I considered this a good thing, and that Roberta's response was that I wasn't enough like him.

She is, of course, correct. He was the most powerful environmental force in my formative (and later) years. As we've discussed, it's your side of the family that causes my inherent personality flaws. My father was a good man; a kind, caring, virtuous man; an intellectually tough and honest man; strong, but not aggressive, insightful without cynicism, an excellent teacher, but not pedantic. He had wisdom. He set a standard that is difficult to meet. I do try to be like him.

Anyway, I've often said that someday I'd write down some of the things he said. I've even called his comments the "Sayings of Chairman Vito." I think now is as good a time as any to try to do that. I don't know where some of these things come from. Some were probably of Italian origin and don't

139

translate well into English. Maybe you can explain. I'm going to try to divide them into categories - to give some order and to help refresh my recollection as I go along.

About Money

The V-man was not concerned about money. My mother has, as far as I know, always handled money matters; he was more inclined to spend it, if he had it, than to worry about getting or keeping it. In general his attitude was:

You can't miss something you never had.

This, of course, applies to many things other than money.

This is not to say that he never talked about it, or its influence on a person's attitude or behavior. In regard to a person's unusual behavior when faced with the possibility of acquiring a rather large sum of money through a questionable transaction, he said:

Money doesn't talk, it screams.

Then there was a similar situation in which a person who would otherwise refrain from acting, just couldn't turn away from the lure of the payoff:

Money talks, nobody walks.

This was used some years ago by a local car dealer in its advertising. More than coincidence? He didn't regard money as good or evil. His attitude was one of neutrality. But he did acknowledge that:

Money is always welcome.

And that:

Whether you're rich or poor, it's nice to have money.

On the other hand, he very clearly felt that money isn't a significant factor in being successful at living a good life:

Money can be too much or too little, but never enough.

I have used this line myself, in what I perceived to be appropriate circumstances. Normally, its use causes a pause and a quizzical face. Some think it doesn't make sense; others find it enigmatic. I don't see the problem.

140

All he meant was that a person can have too much money because it becomes an end in itself and he worries about it; or a person can have too little money and worry about it. But in either case, money won't, in itself, cause a person to suddenly become intelligent, benevolent, loving, lovable or otherwise worthy or content.

In terms of what makes people happy, he believed that wealth had a much broader definition than money. He believed that wealth was in family:

The rich have money; the poor have children.

Roberta and I have a lot of children (and grandchildren). They are all treasures, albeit there are times when I would prefer the silence of money. His background didn't include access to, or the advantages of, money:

When I was a kid, we didn't have two nickels to rub together.

It must have been true. His brother, my uncle Joe, said the same thing. Uncle Joe is noteworthy for other reasons that we needn't get into. My kids remember him as the man who looks like the Indian on the obverse side of the buffalo nickel, which makes the saying somehow more appropriate coming from him. Nor did he feel that his position had changed much since childhood:

If it cost a dollar to send a ton of shit around the world, I couldn't afford to send a fart across the street.

His only financial advice to me was:

It takes money to make money.

Now, this sounds contradictory to some, but it is the best financial advice I know. In my world, at least, if you want to make money, you need to have some first. This you do by that most un-American method - working and saving. But saving isn't enough either since the banking business is premised on the stupidity of the saver (they pay 3% and invest at 8-16%). They are, of course, aided and abetted in their quest to pillage the workingman by the workingman's government, which will give tax breaks to the powerful but refuses to forgive taxes on savings. You have to beat them at their own game. This reminds me of a story which I shall now inflict on you.

A couple of years ago, Roberta and I decided to refinance an investment property (what you would call a tenement). Interest rates had declined to their lowest level in ten years or more and we discerned (by some simple calculations) that we could save (or "earn") some money by refinancing. I dealt with a young man with the title of Vice President. It seems that everyone at a bank (who isn't a teller) is a "vice president." After a lot of paper work (most of which, we were told, was required by the government) it appeared that we had an agreement in principle; i.e., they had decided we were credit worthy. So we got down to the nuts and bolts:

"What term did you want? 25 years?"

"No, I want 10 years. "

"Why do you want that?"

"Don't you own a calculator? Listen, my boy. The longer I stretch out the term of the payments, the more money you make. That is not in my best interest, but yours. Why would I want to make you rich?"

"But most people want low monthly payments."

"Yes, they do. But that's because they can't afford a big monthly payment. I'm not one of those people."

"Oh. So, we'll make it ten years. Now, the closing costs will be about $2,200 and you'll have to bring a check for that amount at closing."

"No I won't."

"Excuse me?"

"I said, 'no I won't.' Get your calculator working, my boy. I want the closing cost rolled into the mortgage amount."

"That's not usually the way it's done. Why do you want to do that?"

"Like I said, get your calculator working. This isn't nuclear physics. This is numbers. Look at it this way: I've got the $2,200. Hell, I could pay this loan off from my checking account [not really, but I was on a roll]. But that money is invested and earning about 13%. Why in the world would I give up a 13% return, when I can use your money at 7.25% with Uncle Sam giving me a deduction for that amount? The point is that I'm going to use your money to make money." [The V-man never said it had to be your own money that you used to make money]

"Gee, I never looked at it that way."

"Maybe you oughta."

Having given the vice president a lesson in basic financing, we put all the papers in order and set a closing date. The morning of the closing (which was set to take place at 10) I received a call from a paralegal with the law firm that was handling the bank's end. She said:

"Mr. Villanova, I think everything is set to go. I remind you, though, that you're supposed to bring a check for $1250."

"I'm not bringing any check."

"But, the bank requires it for real estate tax escrow."

"Not from me they're not. Talk to the guy at the bank and remind him that we agreed there would be no tax escrow."[32]

"OK."

Ten minutes later:

"Mr. Villanova, he said it's a requirement, and that they can't do anything about it."

"Then you tell him that we can forget the whole thing and I'll see him in court."

"I think you should tell him that yourself."

"Yeah. Give me his phone number."

So, I call the bank guy:

"You see, Mr. Villanova, we require escrow on all our mortgages, and we can't make exceptions."

"You made an exception on this one."

"How so?""

"I'm looking at the agreement right now. Get your copy. In the place indicating the amount of escrow it says zero. That's the deal. If you're telling me that it's not the deal, then you're in breach of the agreement and I'm sure the banking commission would be interested in that."

"Well, that's not in accord with our rules."

"I don't give a rat's kiester about your rules. If it's your rule, you can waive it. You are a Vice President, aren't you? Surely you have the authority to waive your own rule."

"Well ... I guess I could."

"Do it. I'll be at your lawyer's office at 11."

I hung up without the normal farewell. Five minutes later the paralegal called again.

"Mr. Villanova, the bank has agreed to waive the escrow."

"Did they now? How Christian of them."

"Uh, yeah. We've rescheduled for 11. OK?"

"Yeah, fine."

"How did you get them to do that?"

"Let's just say they understand that it takes money to make money."

Unkind Remarks

My father was not a man to belittle, criticize or otherwise speak harshly about anyone. However, there were some occasions when the severity of the person's affliction overrode his reluctance to comment.

---

[32] I see no reason for a bank to have my money (and make money on it) for six months, so they can pay my taxes. We're mature responsible adults, we can pay the taxes ourselves, just like we've done for 30 years.

About ugly:

She's as homely as a mud fence.

She had a face that would stop a sundial.

A coat of paint will hide a multitude of sins.

Said of a lady with gobs of make up, but applicable to many other situations.

He's so ugly he hurt my eyes.

About stupidity:

He wouldn't know his ass from a hole in the ground

Thoughts which proceed from the wine-soaked brain.

Said in reference to some inane comments that my mother-in-law had made. Speaking of inane mother-in-law comments, here's a recent exchange between Dot and Roberta:
"I'd like to come noth this summuh."
"Yeah?"
"Somebody will hafta take me though."
"Does 'somebody' have a name?" [when Dot says "somebody" she means Roberta]
"Well, ya could fly down heuh and drive me up theyuh, then drive me back down an' fly back."
"And do you suppose that 'somebody' would pay for the plane tickets, too?"
"Well ...."
"Either you're crazy, or you think I am."
"Maybe it's not such a good idear."

It isn't that I disagree so much as I'm totally disinterested in what he has to say.

One of my favorite lines; a subtle, but marvelous, put down. I don't recall the details. He said this in a way that indicated his total lack of respect for the person's intelligence. He had another way of getting the point across:

This is like abstract art. Unless the guy can paint a horse that looks like a horse, I don't give a shit about his splotches.

Empty vessels resound the loudest.

Said of Lunkhead after he had completed a high volume, bombastic diatribe against then President (old "golf balls in the intestines") Eisenhower.[33]

Little things trouble little minds.

Said of your sister-in-law Julie (you know, Babe) who was fretting about the flaking of her fingernail polish.

More unkind remarks:

He's chewing on the genitals of ant.

and

The apple doesn't fall far from the tree.

An aside to me during a meandering discourse by my cousin Al, a really nice guy but prone to verbosity and not known for eschewing minutiae. His dad, as you know, was the same way.

The Lord knows what he's doing.

Said in response to an inquiry from a child about why Julie and Eddie (you know, Babe and Bobo) didn't have children.

Even a blind pig occasionally finds an acorn.

One of my oft' used favorites. The first time I heard this was circa 1956 when a local, small time, beer befuddled, sand and gravel guy named Willie was cutting some trees for my father. Most of his efforts produced unexpected and occasionally dramatic results, with he and others running in fear lest they be struck by an improperly severed maple. He did, however, succeed in placing one pine where he wanted it, to his (and our) surprise. His obvious glee with this event brought forth the comment from the V-man.

---

[33] President Eisenhower was an avid golfer. Uncle Fred & I were listening to a Red Sox game, when it was interrupted by a news flash that the President had been hospitalized with "ileitis." I asked what that meant. Uncle Fred immediately said, "golf balls in the intestines." It's some sort of intestinal inflammation.

Life &Death

His attitude toward both life and death was virtually the same.

Life is too serious to take seriously.

and

When I die the world dies with me.

Taken together, these concepts indicate an attitude of (sometimes be-mused) detachment that allows a less emotional perspective on day-to-day tribulations that can, without such detachment, engulf one in a sea of angst. Better to take on the attitude of an observer than a participant. Better to look for balance.

His attitude toward other people was almost uniformly benevolent and patient. However, if another person had a problem dealing with him, he shrugged it off:

To hell with those who hate me.

This is his English version of an Italian saying which, rendered in type phonetically, would be something like "ah fache key mu mal." It is similar to the expression I hear as *a face da sordela*, or *sordeda,* but which would be "to the face [*alla face*] of your sister [*della tua sorella*]." "Your sister's face???" What the hell is that supposed to mean anyway? Can you tell me how to say, "to hell with those who hate me" in real Italian?

Or:

They can kiss my dago ass.

An expression I use so often that some of my colleagues are in the habit of saying, "As Villanova would say - KMDA."

About getting old

If you live long enough, you get old.

Said in response to a statement, made in jest, which implied that his age was somehow a matter that could be controlled.

Getting old isn't for sissies.

Said in response to a rather flattering comment about his robust physical condition.

Life's a bitch, but consider the alternative.

Said in response to a series of whining, negative comments, about I don't know what, from Hilda.

Nobody gets out of this alive.

Said in response to the report of a number of people killed in an airplane mishap.

We're all going to the same place.

Said in regard to the comments of a hyped-up, sophomoric overachiever.

I don't need a doctor to help me die.

Said in response to my strong suggestion (I never, ever, told my father to do anything) that he seek professional medical advice.

As long as you're hurting, you know you're alive.

Said to me after I complained of pain associated with a broken knee, and absolutely right. The times I've been in serious trouble, it didn't hurt.

Rules to Live By

Despite all the blathering about popular psychology, from Joyce Brothers to the shallow, empty headed tripe viewed daily by millions who watch Donahue, Oprah, et. al., I think the best advice I've heard about the rules of engagement for life came from my father. He never once used the phrase "self esteem" either. His advice was direct, simple and accurate.

The helping hand you're looking for is at the end of your arm.

This is, I believe, the single most profound and valuable piece of advice I have ever received or given. It embodies the essence of personal freedom.

Growing up with this rule has made me impatient and intolerant of any suggestion that the cause of one's difficulties, or the source of their resolution, is "out there" somewhere. If I (or anyone else for that matter) want to see the source of my problems (or their solution) all I need do is look in the mirror. No one "out there" made me the asshole that I am, and no one "out there" is going to save me. All this liberal claptrap about blaming society is unmitigated cow cookies. Of course, blaming society is a self-serving device and, thus, understandable. It's an excuse to make government bigger, more intrusive, more unresponsive to individuals qua individuals. The politicians, the bureaucrats, the doctors, the psychologists, the sociologists, the educationists, and all the other entrenched economic interests would have no power (economic or otherwise) if individuals acknowledged accountability for their own situation and had the intelligence to do something to improve it. But that's not going to happen, is it?

So everyone is a "victim." Even criminals. No? How would you explain the likes of the Menendez boys and Lorena Bobbit? Easy, if everyone is responsible (aka "society") then no one is responsible. This is where liberalism gets us: the denial of personal accountability leads to the abdication of personal freedom. The miscreant "had no choice" but to kill his parents or cut off the offending appendage, or steal to support his habit, etc., etc. This is bullshit. But they "couldn't help it." Couldn't they?

We've come to the point (as most decadent societies do) where the individual can be persuaded that he cannot handle life on his own; he's a victim of the nameless, faceless, ubiquitous "them." He needs help (e.g., welfare, psychologists, ministers, bureaucrats). So when he fails, it isn't his fault, someone else has failed him. He's got some sort of disability; he's a junkie, an alcoholic, comes from a dysfunctional family; he's an Afro-American, Asian, Indian, Hispanic; he's poor, illiterate, stupid; he was an orphan, abused, grossly obese, anorexic, short, bald, has eleven fingers; whatever. You think I'm exaggerating?

Recently a national news service carried the story of a government employee who was always late to work. So late, in fact, that he sometimes showed up as his co-workers were getting ready to close up for the day. Talk about late. Was he fired? Of course not. He was suffering from a disability, "chronic tardiness syndrome," so he was placed on medical disability leave (with pay, of course). What nonsense.

Everybody has a story. Most of our failures are simply failures of our own will. I ought to know; I'm still smoking. The helping hand you're looking for is at the end of your arm.

If you're looking for sympathy you'll find it in the dictionary, right after shit.

This is a corollary of the preceding rule. It sounds harsh, but I didn't include it under Unkind Remarks because it is not meant to be unkind. It was always said in the manner of "what do you want from me?" Sympathy is a nice human emotion, but what does it do? It usually doesn't burden the giver by giving it, and it does nothing to improve the lot of the recipient. It's something that is productive of nothing; i.e., shit.

It's not the thing that's important; it's the doing of the thing that's important.

Whatever he was doing, my father did it with enthusiasm and the right way – no shortcuts. But he wasn't attached to the finished product once it was done, nor looking for any sort of recognition or reward for having done it. The significance of the action was in the action itself. He enjoyed the "coming into being" of the activity. Once it was done, he'd find something else to do.

The wiser bends.

and

Don't stiffen up, you'll break.

My father didn't see the world or his place in it in terms of absolutes. Very few things were black or white, but infinite shadings of gray. He, thus, adopted a flexible, calm and responsive approach to the ever-changing vagaries of normal life. He equated rigidity in thought and action with stupidity because only stupidity could explain a lack of awareness of the fact that facts change. Non - recognition of the inherent instability of future circumstances, to him, disclosed a lack of intelligence and a recipe for continuous disappointment.

This attitude leads to his conclusion that:

Everything is adjustable; life itself is adjustable.

Actually, he first said this to me while we were pondering together over a design problem in one of his innumerable woodworking projects. His solution, in which I concurred, was to adjust the design to avoid the problem. The maxim, clearly, has a much broader application than the particular issue we were then addressing. It applies to life. I've used the principle in dealing with "personnel problems." I think you know that for many years I was responsible for the paralegals and the paralegal program at my former employer. I periodically spoke to them *en masse*, normally including comments along the following lines:

"I am aware of an undercurrent of residual discontent with certain aspects of your situation here. This discontent is more acute for some of you than for others. That fact notwithstanding, my advice to you all is this. In any situation (here or in the real world) you essentially have three options. One, you can suffer in silence; grin and bear it; and just grit it out. Two, you can take some responsibility for the situation and work within it to make it more to your liking. I will do my best to help you to make changes that I think are appropriate under all the facts and circumstances, but it is you who must identify the problem and suggest remedies. And third, you can extract yourself from the situation. After all, you were looking for a job when you found this one, weren't you? For my part, if you choose the third option, I will not be offended. To me, you are all fungible, like the tires on my car. If you wear out, or blowout, I'll get another one that looks just like you. That door swings both ways; don't let it hit you in the butt on the way out."

This became known as the "door swings both ways" speech, which some of the paralegals (the good ones) suggested I just put on tape and show to new people so they wouldn't have to listen to it anymore. Sounds pretty obnoxious, doesn't it? But I always delivered the speech with tone, inflection and gesture intended to convey my genuine affection for them and concern about their particular situations. Despite the rather generous authority granted to me in paralegal matters, there were limitations on my ability to make an ideal work world for each of them. A certain amount of whining and sniveling is normal and expected, but it's sometimes just impossible to satisfy some people. For such people, it is best that they move on, for their own sake, and for the sake of those that want to stay.

Far be it from me to stand in their way.

My father was a careful planner; he was of the "measure twice - cut once" school. But the plan was not allowed to become something in itself; it was always just a prediction:

A plan isn't real; it's just an idea. Don't make yourself crazy; let it evolve.

I received this advice during a discussion about a grandmother clock I was making for Rhonda. I had no plans, just pictures of several different cases each of which had some features I liked (and some I didn't). I skipped the plan stage altogether and just let it evolve. It came out nice.

Again, however, the advice applies to much more than cabinetry. Many times in my previous working life, I was faced with detailed plans created by people who believed that the plan was real. Some of these were simply impossible to implement as written because reality couldn't be changed to suit the plan. Others led their authors to untold anxiety and disappointment,

150

sometimes failure, because they believed the plan stated what will be, rather than understanding that it was only a prediction about what might be, if we played our cards right and circumstances didn't change. But circumstances almost always change. It isn't humanly possible to anticipate all the possible changes or to control the actions of others or future events. Whenever I was involved in planning, I made sure that any written plan was chock full of weasel words which would grant the maximum amount of discretion to modify, amend, or otherwise adjust the plan to account for changing circumstances, or terminate it.

More About Planning

If you don't know what to do, don't do anything.

Good advice. This remark was prompted by some idiot politician who was pressing to enact a piece of legislation the consequences of which he admittedly could not foresee. Nevertheless, he believed that he had to do something, anything, in the hope that his constituents would mistake movement for progress. My father maintained that in most situations in which one doesn't know what to do, the uncertainty is caused by insufficient, incomplete, or unreliable information. Better to do nothing until you know the facts. But sometimes it's best to do nothing even if you know all the facts:

A master stays his hand and allows the situation to work itself out.

I don't remember the circumstances that caused this comment. The gist of its meaning, however, is that an astute planner will not interfere with or push the progression of the plan (or the situation) if it is evolving toward the intended result of its own momentum. I have used this "hands off" approach in any number of situations that were more matters for mediation than advocacy. Sometimes, when you let the actors play out the roles themselves, they think they did it themselves, and each goes away pleased. Litigation is not an efficient form of dispute resolution, and the less the lawyers interfere, the less the likelihood of litigation. Of course, there are times when a gentle nudge, a subtle cue or a mild suggestion can channel the flow of events in a positive direction, but that can be done without the appearance of advocacy or demand.

Yet,

Deciding to do nothing is itself a decision.

The key is that the doing of nothing is the product of a conscious decision - a choice - made after consideration and analysis of all the available

151

information. Such a decision, according to the V - man, is not a negation of the power to choose, but an affirmation of it.

Don't muddy the water; you'll end up drinking it.

I don't recall the reason for this remark. The intendment, I do recall: think before you stir up trouble, you'll have to deal with the consequences. Think about it before you act:

Never say anything behind someone's back that you haven't already said to his face.

I have uniformly and consistently adhered to this bit of doctrine. First, because I think it's cowardly to denigrate someone who isn't there to defend himself. Second, because having already made the object of your criticism aware of the criticism, it comes as no surprise if he hears of your opinion from another. This cannot hurt you in the eyes of the object of your critique; indeed, he might respect you for telling him first; and the gossip he hears it from will be defused in his effort to cause you grief.

Better the devil you know than the devil you don't know.

Applied to any situation in which a change is being proposed without full information about, or full consideration of all the information pertaining to, the proposed change (e.g., job change, residence change, spouse change) usually where the reasons for the proposed change have the appearance of running away from the issues rather than trying to face them.

You mess with the bull; you get the horns.

Said on virtually every occasion where the result of my, or someone's, carelessness caused injury. The "bull" could be anything that is dangerous, either in itself (like a table saw) or the use to which it was put (like a chair instead of a ladder) or just because of the situation (like saying something nasty to someone named Luigi).

Even a dog knows the difference between being stumbled over and kicked.

Said in reference to some particularly unkind remarks by Hilda in the presence of and at the expense of Julie; followed by the former's assertion of jovial intent (we know better, don't we).

Others

I'll lump some others together.

Yeah, and if the dog didn't stop to shit, maybe he would've caught the rabbit.

My father was not one to bemoan his fate or otherwise speculate about what might have been. He never used the words "would have - could have - should have" in any context indicating disappointment or displeasure with something that might have been, "if" or "if only" something had or had not happened. Moreover, he didn't take well to those who did, which is the reason he used this pithy conversation stopper.

Untested virtue is no virtue at all.

A comment prompted by the televised discourse of a catholic priest concerning the virtue of marital fidelity, something the V - man agreed with completely. But, hey, if you don't have the experience of participating in the game, you shouldn't do the play by play. More broadly, he said that having a code of conduct doesn't mean anything unless you live by it.

And one bit of wisdom with which you will wholeheartedly agree:

Don't take any shit from anybody.

This seems a belligerent statement.

I don't have memories that would indicate that my father was a belligerent man. I, of course, didn't know him as a young person and I suspect that a portion of his youth was misspent. After all, a guy with his looks, build, and attitude hanging around with the guys he hung out with, must have been in a few scrapes. I don't have any distinct memory of overt belligerence except for a foggy recollection of a roadway incident.

As best I can bring it back, I was in the rear seat of a '39 Oldsmobile. Another car (it looked like Uncle Roger's Plymouth business coupe) almost forced us off the road. My father somehow caught and made the other guy stop. He went over to the other car with a tire iron in his hand. The other guy wouldn't get out of his car to receive his punishment. He had locked his door and rolled up his window, but my father grabbed hold of him through the vent window. There was a stream of accusatory profanity, but the only words I clearly remember were, "Get out of that car or I'm gonna pull your whole pig body through this friggin' vent!"

At the time I thought he could actually do it (he was one tough cookie) but though he tried several times, he couldn't get the guy's head through the narrow space. After a while, he gave up and came back to our car. *"Sfacime"*[34] he said, "I don't take any shit from anybody" and that was the end of it. We continued on our way to get some New York system hot wieners in Olneyville. He didn't seem angry or upset; he wasn't breathing hard or muttering. In fact, he didn't tell my mother about the incident, and it was never mentioned thereafter. It was just something he had to do, no big deal.

I took it that for him it was a matter of principle; he wasn't acting out of anger, but a sense of duty; a duty to himself. He couldn't let a wrong pass. He wouldn't be victimized.

That's about all I can put together. There are probably some I've overlooked. But just going back and reading this thing before I send it to you makes me realize that my father gave me a priceless legacy; one I wasn't fully aware of and didn't fully appreciate until now. His sayings and his actions are expressions of a deep wisdom that made him a good man and a great father.

He's a tough act to follow; he was good at life. I think his mother named him right.

Anyway, [topic jump] I've reminded Darlene (aka "Dolly") that she "owes" you a response of some sort to your last rambling, semi-coherent, letter. (I'm just fooling around; lighten up).

[Another topic jump] Oh yeah, by the way, you were right. The identity of the people in the old photograph we talked about has been determined. It's a picture of some of your grandparents; i.e., your mother's mother and father; with your mother's sister (Alvera?), Uncle Red and another, very tall (& blind?) brother, whose name has escaped me as I type this. I can remember things that happened almost 50 years ago, but can't remember something I was told last weekend.[35] Oh well, getting old isn't for sissies.

Roberta and I, and my entire family, send our love to you and Aunt Virginia. Rhonda acknowledges, with particular affection for you, your congratulations and best wishes on the birth of Daron (I swear he has the same semi-demonic, glint in his eyes that you have. He looks like you. I'm absolutely serious).

---

[34] SOB

[35] Uncle Fred's mother was Carmella (nee Villela); his father was Francesco (Cheech). Uncle Red – Ernest Villela, called "Red" because his hair was red. Grampa Cheech called him *il lupo* (the wolf) because he was hairy all over. I think Gramma Gabriele's other brother was Louie. He was taller than Uncle Red by 3 or 4 inches, which means that he was about 6' 5" – very unusual for his generation.

Qualiscumque

Dear Uncle Fred,

O kay. You've had sufficient respite from my written ramblings. It is time for another semi-coherent, probably disconnected, series of comments, questions and tall tales.

Roberta and I recently returned from yet another trip to our place in Florida. Before you feel envy, remember that my mother-in-law lives in FL, and that she is ensconced a mere 3 miles away from our place. I have previously indicated that the relationship between us is sometimes less than cordial. There are many reasons for that, but it is enough to say that I don't like her and she doesn't like me. That mutual feeling does not, however, prevent her from presuming that she can ask me to perform maintenance tasks in and around her dwelling each time I am in town. In fact, before we arrive she makes a list (I'm not kidding) of those things she wants done while I'm there.

She is presumptuous. This attitude is born of a belief that she is the center of the universe and that no person or event has any significance except as it relates to her needs and wants. I know of no other person more self-centered and self-absorbed. I may have already told you this story, but I'll repeat it just to give you one example that proves my point.

Roberta's father was very ill. A doctor was explaining to us (i.e., Dot, Roberta & me) that her Dad was not likely to recover. He had barely finished, when Dot said, "Yeah, but what about me?" The doctor was dumbstruck; Roberta was dumbstruck; I was not surprised.

Anyway, few of these tasks are demanding. For example, I have fixed plumbing, installed ceiling fans and light fixtures, changed the water filter, fixed a flat tire, put water in her water bed, evicted ants from the water heater and adjusted the heater's temperature, figured out and filed her taxes, and stuff like that. There are some tasks, however, that I am unwilling to perform. For example, she had it in her mind that I would climb on the roof of her garage with a chain saw and cut off a limb that extended over the house. To me, this seemed at best a recipe for a trip to the emergency room. I declined this task, explaining that I am 56 years old, and do not voluntarily clamber on roofs, let alone with chain saw in hand.

Dot said, "Well, what am I gonna do?" I said, "Before you ask me to do anything I want you to ask yourself this question, "What would I do if Ronnie were dead? Do you understand? What would you do if I were dead?"

155

"Well, I don' know."

"Think about it. What would you do?"

"Well, I guess I'd ask somebody else ta do it."

"Or?"

"Huh?"

"Or, what else?"

"I don't know."

"How about calling someone who does it for a living?"

"Huh? Ya mean pay somebody tuh do it?"

"Bingo."

"I'd rather let the tree fall on the house. Then the insurance would pay."

Roberta says that this was a clever ruse by her mother, designed to precipitate my fall from the roof. I might buy that if I thought her mother were capable of a clever ruse, or a clever anything, for that matter. The woman can't even conjugate verbs. This is an actual bit of conversation (I wrote it down):

"Ya know, Doris come ovuh yestuhday, an' an' ... She had it with her. An, an, when Tony come ovuh, he said he didn't know anythin' about it."

"You mean came."

"Huh?"

"You mean he came over, past tense."

"Huh?"

"When did Doris and Tony arrive here?"

"Hell, I don' know. Maybe las' Thursday."

"Well, whether it was a minute ago, a week ago or a year ago, they came in the past. The past tense of the verb 'to come' is 'came.' 'Come' is usually present or future. Like 'come here', or 'when does the garbage man come?'"

"Ah, jeez. Anyway, when Tony got here........."

I found this response intriguing. First, she didn't say "When Tony get here." Second, she had the capacity to avoid the criticism by selecting an alternate verb. I listened for verb tense usage and found that the only deviation from conventional temporal tense usage is "come." Odd, don't you think? I started listening for other deviations. I found nothing unusual, other than the normal dialectic eccentricities of a New England upbringing; like saying "I guess" for "I think," "dinner" for the noon-time meal and "supper" for the evening meal, "cabinet" for milkshake, "eaves trough" for gutter (which she wanted me to clean - I didn't).

Now I'm thinking that maybe this isn't a simple product of ignorance. Maybe something else is at work. What?

I think you'll recall (if you don't you should take more ginko biloba) that Dot is in her seventies, a widow, and has the personality of an ill tempered, bad-mannered child. She is not a person who relates easily with others.

Roberta and her aunt (Helen), who have tolerated more abuse from Dot than a normal person would, have taken on the task of trying to get Dot out of her cigarette-smoke saturated house. I'm sure their intentions in this regard are noble. For my part, it is my (vain) hope that she will tie-up with some dumb bastard who will take her away to his home in some godforsaken state like Montana; maybe North Dakota.

In furtherance of their objective, Roberta and Helen advocate that Dot go to the Senior Center dance on Monday nights. Of course, Dot won't do that on her own, so they tell her that we (Roberta and I) and they (Helen and her spouse, Normand) are going. Norm and Helen are both in their late 70s, are very nice, good-hearted people, and are accomplished ballroom, square and clog dancers. Both Norm and I have been coerced by our respective spouses to dance with Dot on a number of prior occasions (at the Elks and the Senior Center). Both Norm and I have found that experience to be wholly unsatisfactory, bordering on distasteful. I'll tell you why.

Norm and I adopt the traditional starting position; i.e., facing our partner, right hand at partner's waist, left hand holding partner's right hand (relaxed) at partner's shoulder height. Roberta and I have danced together since we were teenagers, so no matter what the beat or tempo we manage a fluid (I'm tempted to say graceful) style. That's what I'm used to. With Dot, it is less like dancing and more like struggling. Dot will not face her partner. Instead she turns away 90 degrees so that her left hip is at a right angle to said partner. She then shoves her left hand, arm fully extended, to the level of the top of her head. Her first move is to step sideways with her right foot (away from her partner) and commence a herky-jerky rocking motion from the waist up.

She will not be led. Any effort by her partner to restrain or redirect either the sideways step or the herky-jerky rocking produces a disproportionate, corresponding counter-movement, which accentuates the herky-jerky action. This results in what I can only describe as a display worthy of St. Vitus in full spasm.

Dot agreed to join us at the Senior Center, in part at least, because on a previous visit she had danced with a guy named Ed. She thought they had danced pretty well together, although "we didn't move much."

The band consisted of five members, none of whom were under the age of 75. They played no tune that post-dated WW II. They were a fair group, and I enjoyed the music. The fact that all of it was more than 50 years old was a pleasant change from the usual fare. A surprising product of that evening is that I discovered that I knew the words to every tune, almost all of which had been written and popular before I was born. A fellow 20 years my senior was singing and looking to me to fill in the gaps in his memory. What's up with that? Did you, my Dad, Uncle Gog, Uncle Ed, teach me the lyrics?

No one danced with Dot. Helen had no success with Norm. Roberta had no success with me. Ed danced often, but not with Dot. Neither Helen and Norm nor Roberta and I danced, because Dot wasn't dancing. Norm introduced me to Ed.

"So, Ed, I understand you've danced with my mother-in-law."

"Oh...uh....yeah. Yeah I did."

"What do you think?"

"Well, … uh...I tried to dance with her. I thought she wanted to lead, so I tried that. But ...uh ... that didn't seem to work, and we just kinda stood in one spot while she rocked. I'm sorry if I offended her by not dancing with her tonight, but ... uh ... I just didn't want to go through that again."

Norm and I said in unison, "We understand."

Now, you may be muttering, why does my nephew constantly regale me with stories about this woman. That's a legitimate question. The answer is really simple, and it is the answer I give Roberta when she wonders aloud why her mother is a common topic of conversation with me and her relatives; Dot is probably the most interesting person we know. I mean, let's face it, most of us are pretty boring. I know I am. Not that boring is a bad thing - I think it's the usual state of the vast majority of people I know - but it doesn't make for lively conversation.

After all, if I wrote to you about what my children are doing, or the cute things my grandchildren did and said, and sent you pictures of us with the grandkids; that would not exactly stimulate your senses or your interest. But talking about Dot and other odd people, people who are different, at least that gets your attention. In fact, anyone can get more attention by being different, particularly if the differences are annoying, than by being bland.

I think I'm basically bland and boring. I have no criminal history. I haven't had as much as a parking ticket, ever. I don't drink, gamble, do drugs, womanize, play sports, sky dive or anything else that would add pepper to a person's existence. My core emotion ranges from lethargy to apathy to ennui. At bottom I just don't care about the world's ills. I don't have the strength to care about anything but my family.

So, Brazil's economy is in the toilet. Some country's economy is always in the toilet. So, they're killing each other in Kosovo. Somebody's always killing somebody for some stupid reason or no reason at all. So they're starving in Rwanda. Somebody's always starving somewhere. So, the President is a scumbag.[36] Some politician is always a scumbag. Don't we pay enough taxes to hire people who do care to handle these things? Goddamit, let them take care of it, shut up, and leave me alone. I don't care; I can't care; I don't have the strength.

On that point, I wish that all those assholes in D.C. would just go home and stay there for at least two years. It's time for all of them to stop legislat-

---

[36] Clinton

ing, investigating, pontificating and, oh yeah, fornicating with the help. And speaking of the president and the pope, why don't those damn fools just step aside - be a man - resign? Sonsabitches. Dirty bastards. They're not worth the space they occupy; get out of the way and let someone else give it a try. Someone else couldn't possibly do worse.

Well, that felt good. What was I saying?

Oh yeah. That was my point, I guess. I'm so boring that I feel obliged to create a different public persona. So I feign irritation, shock, anger and horror at virtually everything. I natter at Roberta and my children just to get their goat and some attention. I speak in exaggeration, hyperbole and metaphor. I go over the top. I make towering figures of evil out of humble miscreants. I decry the state of society, heap wrath on TV personalities, loathing on authorities and pundits. I am the knower of all things. Everyone and everything else is *merde*. I behave like a chrome plated jerk.

You are probably one of the few people I know who can understand what I'm saying. You are probably one of the few who know how much energy is required, how draining it is, to keep up this show, this pretense, of connection with and response to the world. For me, the worst thing that could happen is for someone to know me as bland and boring. It's just such an effort, though. My heart isn't in it. I don't know how long I can keep it up.

Lately, I've been slipping. Lately, I've been thinking that Dot just can't help it. It's not her choice to be what she is. That dancing thing proves she's just not wired-up right.

Lately, I've stopped short of getting Roberta to the point of anger. Lately, I've been telling her I'm just putting her on. Lately, I've been biting my tongue with the children and not shooting out the wise-ass counterpoint. Lately, I've stopped advocating the extermination of the entire human species; nuking the whales; cutting down the rain forest; and mandatory prefrontal lobotomy of liberals.

Lately I've been slipping into a Zen-like state of whateverness. I think I'll miss those outraged, neck throbbing expulsions of vitriolic, obscenity laden, diatribes. But, they just take too much energy. They're getting tired; they're losing their impact; I'm repeating myself; I'm getting tired.

Lately, Roberta has been buying herbs and powdered roots and making my tea. That's nice, don't you think?

Hmmmm. Hey. Whatever. I guess I don't care.

Call me, dammit. If you saw my last phone bill, you'd think I was the Bank of America.

Love to you and Aunt Virginia.

The Uncertainty Principle

Dear Uncle Fred,

It's been more than a few months since I assailed you with one of these tedious exercises. I trust you are in the mood for more nonsense, so I'll entertain you with some commentary and stories which may or may not be connected in the real world but which are related in the netherworld of my mind.

I started writing this (literally writing - I don't take this machine with me) while we were in Florida (about six months ago). As you know, Roberta and I try to spend the winter months out of the gray-cold belt of New England. Many people seem envious of this practice. There is some reason for that, but as with most life circumstances, there are down sides to the obvious benefits of staying climactically comfortable between the equinoxes. Before I get to that, though, I want to tell you that during December we were joined by la Giaponese, the Patra and Paul.

That visit was noteworthy in some respects. For example, it marked the first time that my mother traveled by plane; the first time she visited Florida; the first time she saw our winter home (we've been there for 8 years) and the first time she experienced the Magic Kingdom and Epcot. Not a bad list of firsts for someone as old as a redwood.

Ever think about that? You're older than most trees. So am I, and I intend to become much, much older. I am already a cantankerous old fart according to some. I don't see it that way of course, I'm just trying to have some fun. I've worked long and hard to get to this position in life; to wit, I don't owe anybody anything. I don't have to be nice, I don't have to be agreeable, I don't have to be sensitive, I don't have to be considerate, kind, diplomatic, politic or politically correct. I'm not afraid of life or death. I don't have to put up with shit from anybody. Of course, I am (most of the time) considerate, kind, and all those other warm, fuzzy things. But the point is that I don't have to be. It's my choice.

Anyway, for various reasons I have recently been asked what I do, the implication being that because I have chosen not to work I must have a ton of time on my hands. Well, I've got news for them (and you) I'm busier than the proverbial one-armed paperhanger. Obviously, you know by the lengthy gap between letters that I don't spend every day writing these silly letters. In addition to writing other silly letters and a veritable plethora of manual activities, I read. Yes, I read books. Hard-covered books with lots of pages, densely packed words, no photos of handsome young people with perfect teeth distracting attention by shallow titillating symbol from the *jejeune* narrative they interrupt. I read non-fiction, unpopular works like history, law, economics, archaeology, dead languages, mythology and physics.

Physics? Yeah, physics.

In high school, I took physics because I had to. I didn't like it. I didn't understand it and didn't care to understand it. All those nuclei and electrons, those atoms, molecules and stuff whizzing around just didn't interest me. Who cares how many protons an atom has? Who cares how many angels can dance on the head of a pin? I don't. So why, you should be asking, this late blooming interest in physics? That will take some explaining.

In a nutshell, it went like this. Ever since grammar school I've had a keen interest in anything to do with ancient Egypt and Mesopotamia. This has led to an intractable problem. There is no dearth of information available about these ancient civilizations. But the information is collected, analyzed and interpreted through the modern eyes of specialists whose specialities are so narrow (though they don't see it this way) that what you get is a thorough description of artifacts, but virtually no credible explanation of meaning.

This is not their fault. Western analytical processes have been dominated for too long by reductionists. We believe that the perfect scientific method is to chop the thing under study into the smallest possible parts. Then we scrutinize each part individually, chop it into yet smaller parts and scrutinize those parts. When we have chopped as fine as our wit allows and gathered all the data on the miniscule severed members of the thing, we "know" it. Thus an expert has been defined (I don't know who came up with this definition) as a person who learns more and more about less and less until he knows absolutely everything about nothing.

More crudely, but more quaintly I think, reductionists are like the Fugarwe bird - a mythic avis that flies in circles of ever decreasing radii until its head is up its anus; which is particularly apt because that is where the heads of most experts are.

After much reading, I concluded that there is an untapped source of astronomical information in ancient Egyptian texts. The Egyptians and the Sumerians (the Chinese, and much later the Maya) were absolutely bonkers about astronomy. However, often the translation of the ancient texts renders the script literally and is thereby made wholly devoid of meaning. In an effort to confirm that this is the case, I began reading some fairly obscure stuff focusing on ancient astronomies and languages. In one of those works, the author mentioned (for a reason which now escapes me) something called The Uncertainty Principle

What the hell?

Now, I'm as uncertain as a guy can be. In fact, I've done a complete reversal from my young days. When I was young, I knew the answers. If you wanted to know something, just ask me, I had the answer. As I got older, I came to see that I didn't have all the answers, although I still had a handle on the fair majority. Later, I realized that not only did I not know all the answers; I didn't have any answers that I could pronounce with confidence. Still later, I came to the realization that I probably didn't understand the questions; let alone what the answers might be. I am now of a mind that I have not a single answer, that I don't understand the questions that are asked, and that I have no idea of what the right questions would be, or indeed whether there are any valid questions. So when I read that uncertainty had been (without my knowledge of course) ennobled to the level of a principle, well I just had to find out why.

It turns out that a fellow named Heisenberg made uncertainty a principle. He had to. He was messing around, trying to measure the velocity and location of some subatomic thingamajig or other, when he realized that he could measure velocity, or he could measure place, but couldn't measure both at once. More distressing (apparently) was the depressing realization that as he tried to do his measurements it was obvious that the mere fact of observation affected the thing observed. Thus, he knew what it was doing when he looked at it, but didn't have a clue about what it was doing (if anything) when he wasn't. Further reading disclosed that the very best minds this planet has to offer don't know whether those subatomic whatchamacallits are particles, waves or something else.

When they look for a wave they find something that acts like a wave, and when they look for a particle, sure enough, that same thing acts like a particle. Some have hypothesized that what the thing "is" depends on what the observer thinks it is. Others theorize that whatever "it" is, it is (1) neither a particle nor a wave, or (2) both a particle and a wave until someone observes "it" and by the act of observation "collapses" all the possibilities into a single reality. Still others theorize that the "thing" is not a point particle at all, but an incredibly small, vibrating, two dimensional, "string."

All this sounds more like Hindu/Buddhist philosophy than science. It is farfetched enough to be summarily dismissed as foolishness having nothing to do with the hard reality of life if it were not for the fact that so many of the things that surround us and that we use everyday (like this thing I'm typing on now) are the product of mathematical constructs developed in the study of quantum mechanics. Quantum mechanics is grounded on the uncertainty principle. If it weren't for the various mathematical machinations that brainy people have gone through trying to explain how invisible things work, there would be no high tech anything.

I find this amazing and baffling. Good thing I don't need to know why this machine works, just how to use it.

And if the uncertainty principle itself isn't enough to make you wonder what you can know about anything, let me tell you something else I picked up. You were probably taught, I was taught, my children were taught, and my grandchildren are being taught, that electrons are bits of something that circle the nucleus (an aggregate of something called quarks) of an atom like the planets circle the sun. What a pretty picture. The world of the very small and the world of the very large preserve a constancy of order. It turns out that's just baloney.

Speaking of bologna, my high school physics teacher was Mr. DeLatte. My few recollections of his physics class include the following:

(1) He had a slight accent (sort of a Sylvester Stallone type) and a habit. He said, "ya know" often. In this trait he anticipated the current teenage dialect by about 35 years, a dubious distinction. He said "ya know" the way other people say "uh" to pause without breaking the audio trail while thinking of what to say next. I don't know who started this, but someone began to count the number of times "ya know" was uttered. At first, the count was *sotto voce*[37] and singular. However, the count caught the attention of others proximate to the counter because others were not paying attention to DeLatte. Soon more voices picked up the count, the additional voices amplifying the volume level, "six ... seven ... eight ... nine ... ten," until DeLatte could no longer ignore either the chorus or the tittering that accompanied it.

"Ay! Whaddarya doin'? What is that? Huh? Are ya learnin' how to count? Whatsamata with you people? Somethin' funny is going' on here, ... ya know [eleven]. You people, ... ya know, [twelve]...you're not payin' attention. I just said that NO2 is a stable molecule, right Wright." [Ken Wright, a friend of mine]

"Right, Mr. DeLatte."

---

[37] Whispered. Literally – under voice.

"WRONG, Wright. Ya know [thirteen] ... I tol' ya. ... You people aren't payin' attention. How you gonna learn this stuff if ya don' pay attention? ... Ya know? [fourteen] You want me to get angry?"

"... Hey! What is that?"

2) A girl named Carrie something was in the class. She was fairly nondescript: shoulder length brown hair, usual 50's teenage get up, nothing remarkable. One day Carrie showed up with her hair cut short and peroxided blonde (that era's equivalent of this era's nose piercing, I suppose). DeLatte noticed immediately, but said nothing. He paced back and forth, head down, occasionally giving the appearance of raising his eyes to heaven. This went on for a few minutes. Suddenly he stopped, facing and staring out the window. "Carrie," he said, "I know a girl who dyed her hair once. ... Ya know what happen'? ... She turn' out bad!"

Anyway, our teachers (then and now) have been teaching a myth. Whether through ignorance or through compassion for the simple-minded students isn't the point. The point is that throughout this century it has been known that this picture of the very small world isn't right. It is a gross oversimplification, a metaphor at best. The fact is that no one knows what a nucleus looks like or what it's made of, or how the electrons behave. The point is this: if they lied to us about this, what else have they lied about? Our grandchildren are still being taught Newtonian physics as if it were the final word, when we know that the clockwork universe has been discarded by generations of cognoscenti[38] and the latest word from quantum mechanics is that we not only don't know, but we can't know how things work at the subatomic level or what those things are.

But for me, the overriding significance of the uncertainty principle is this: if we can't be certain about what the very building blocks (subatomic particles, waves, strings or whatever) of reality are, then *a fortiori*[39] we can't be certain that our perception of reality is valid, or that there is a reality that we *can* know. You may think this discussion is boring and irrelevant. You may be right. Nevertheless, the uncertainty principle applies to the macro as well as the micro world, and applies in spades to the life experience, as I shall now demonstrate.

Several pages ago I told you that my mother, sister and brother-in-law visited us in Florida. What I didn't tell you then, and will tell you now, is that the uncertainty principle was in full force and effect around the time of that visit. Roberta and I arrived at approximately 11:40 p.m., five days before our guests were due. I unlocked the front door, pushed it open, reached back for the two suitcases I had carried there and stepped into the foyer. There was an unpleasant, damp odor. As I stepped to the hall, I heard "squish." Uh-oh. I turned on some lights. Roberta was still in the van watching Letterman do the Top Ten List. I went out and told her we had a problem.

---

[38] Those who know
[39] With greater strength

The problem was this: inside the toilet tank is a mechanism that senses the water level. Below a fixed point, it allows a valve to open and water enters the tank until a maximum level is reached, at which point the valve closes. This mechanism is, I thought, completely constructed of plastic. What I didn't know, is that one piece is made of steel - the threaded portion of the water level adjustment screw. While we were away (not watching) this screw corroded and failed. Free from the constraint of adjustment, the little valve did what it was supposed to do. It allowed water into the tank.

The tank has a sort of fail-safe system. A standpipe sits in the middle of the tank. One of its functions is to drain away excess water down the sewer pipe if the water level gets too high. Unfortunately, the tank was mounted on the toilet at a slight tilt. This tilt was enough to cause the water to reach the flush handle opening just before it could reach the lip of the standpipe. The result is that water which should have drained away, exited instead through the handle opening, onto the bathroom floor, into the hall, three bedrooms, the den and the foyer. It was decidedly unpleasant.

I stopped the flow of water. We did as much that night as our bodies would allow. Next day we made telephone calls, cleaned, other people showed up. They vacuumed water by the tank full. The rugs were lifted up and huge fans were placed to dry the remaining moisture. I contacted our insurance company. They were not happy to hear from me. They jerked me around for two days before a contractor of their choosing showed up to assess the damage.

The consensus was that the rug in the hall, den, and foyer should be replaced. This seemed a simple, expedient solution. However, since the foyer is contiguous with the living room and there is no way to match a new rug to the old, it was suggested that that rug be replaced as well, even though it was not seriously damaged. So far so good, but the uncertainty principle insinuated itself into the situation by reason of the fact that under part of the foyer, and all the den, was a real parquet oak floor. I did not know of its existence until then. For all I know it didn't exist until we looked at it.

Impregnated with water, the wood had swelled, buckled, and warped. It was unfixable, but replaceable. I decided that I would forego the replacement of the oak in return for the insurer's consent to pay for replacement of the living room rug. After all, that replacement would be far less expensive than replacement of the oak. So I called the adjuster.

"Hello, Lisa. Look, there is a new development. There's an oak parquet floor under the rug in the foyer and den. It's ruined."

"Oh, you didn't tell me that before."

"I didn't know it before. I know it now. That's why I'm telling you now. Anyway, instead of replacing that oak floor, I'm willing to save you some money by foregoing its replacement if you'll agree to replace the living room rug."

"Huh? You can't have both."

"What do you mean both?"

"Well, uh, you can't have the rug and the floor. What rug are you talking about? Where the floor is?"

"That's not what I'm saying. I don't want both. I don't care about replacing the parquet floor. I didn't even know it was there. I'm saying forget the parquet floor - it would cost twice as much as a rug - but pay for replacing the living room rug instead."

"I don't know. We'll pay for replacing the parquet or the rug, but you can't have both."

"Why do you keep saying that? I'm not asking for both a rug and a parquet floor. I'm saying I'll trade you the high cost of a new parquet floor for the low cost of a rug in the living room."

"But why do you want that? Isn't that rug OK?"

"It's not OK because your contractor says there's no way to match the color of the new foyer rug with the existing living room rug."

"So?"

"So? Whaddaya mean, 'so'? Would you want to look at rugs of different shades running through the middle of your house?"

"Well, I don't know."

"Well, I do. You wouldn't. I don't! What is your problem? Don't you see that this is less costly to you?"

"Well, I'll have to talk to my supervisor. I know you can't have both."

"Lisa, I don't mean to hurt your feelings, but maybe you'd better talk to your supervisor because if you say I 'can't have both' one more time I'm going to come right through this phone and get you. You want me to get angry? I say again: I don't want both. I just want a rug! Understand?"

"Well, I think so."

There were three more conversations with Lisa before the affair was settled. I wrote a letter that spelled out our agreement and indicated that if they did "not perform pursuant to the agreement I would ask the Florida Insurance Commissioner to demand that they show cause why their license to do business should not be suspended." This seemed to terminate the matter. Of course by that time - some two months later - all the repairs had long since been completed.

In the meantime, however, we realized that the dampness in the bedroom rugs had been wicked up into the platforms of the waterbeds in two of those rooms. The "pedestals" are made of particleboard. They soaked up the water like a sponge and when the boys tried to lift them to suck up the water, parts of the pedestals collapsed. The result was that we did not have beds for the guests who would be arriving in three days.

I called a local furniture store; told them of the situation; requested new pedestals of solid wood; demanded assurance that they would arrive when the fans were removed; and told them that I would telephone the day before said fans were removed. On that day I spoke with the fan guys. They assured me that they would be in my house promptly at 9 a.m. next day and would finish their task within an hour. I called the pedestal guy and advised him of same, again asking assurance that he would arrive at 10 a.m. "No problem, I'll be there," he said.

Next day, the fan guys showed up at 9:30 a.m., just after I called their office to find out where they were. I immediately called the pedestal guy.

"Hi, is this Evan?"

"Who?"

"Evan."

"No, do you wanna talk to Evan?"

"If he's there, yeah."

"He's not here."

"If he's not there I guess I can't talk to him, eh? Do you know where he is?"

"I'm not sure."

"Well, he's supposed to be heading to my house with a couple of water-bed pedestals. Does that give you any clue?"

"Uh, lemme see. I got the schedule here somewheres - hol' on a minute. [long pause] Hello? Yeah, I got the schedule but I don' see anythin' about pedestals on it. Where's he s'posed ta be at?" ["s'posed to be at"??!!]

"He's supposed to be at 711 Lemon Ave. Is there any way you can get hold of him?"

"Well, uh … yeah … I guess so."

""Please do get a hold of him, and tell him that he's supposed to be here with two pedestals at 10 o'clock. That's ten minutes from now. [long pause] Do you understand what I just said?"

"Uh … yeah … OK … Yeah, ah'll get aholt a him and make sure he knows."

Great. I don't know where Evan is "at" and I don't know his velocity either. I don't know where "at" or how fast my pedestals are traveling. I know that my mother, sister and brother-in-law are in a plane, but I don't know how fast they're going or the plane's location. I do know where the fan guys are and I know their speed; to wit, in my house and dead slow, respectively.

As my morning unfolded, 1300 miles to the north my brother the Me was putting said relatives on an Airtran, non-stop flight from Greene to Orlando. I do mean "putting" them on. He insisted on walking them through the airport, through the gate, out onto the tarmac and to the door of the plane. He gave explicit repeated instructions to Patra to make sure Ma ate, along with sundry other advice pertaining to planes, airports, luggage, the necessity of telephonic communication. In general, he demonstrated an overarching anal retentiveness, which seems to be the curse of a first-born son. Haven't they ever heard of the uncertainty principle?

The fan guys leave; the rug guys disinfect and deodorize the remaining rugs and the furniture. I can't decide whether the damp mildew odor or the chemical odor is worse. Whatever. There is no sign of Evan. However, at 11 o'clock Evan calls; says he's sorry; says he'll be right over; says we're all set; he can be done by 12.

At 11:30, Evan's whereabouts and velocity unknown, I call Roberta's cousin (Beth) and ask that her husband (Lou) house-sit for me so I can go to the airport. She says (without consulting him of course) he'll be happy to oblige. I was not certain that he would be "happy" to come over, but I was certain he would come over. Beth (like her cousin) is a "she who must be obeyed." Now, it happened that certain of Beth's kin were arriving on the same plane as my relatives and that Beth's parents were going to pick them up. We decided to attempt to restrict the parameter of uncertainty, so Roberta went with her aunt while I waited for Lou; or Evan; or Lou and Evan; or whatever. Lou arrived. I head to the airport, still uncertain that the arrivals will have a place to lay their heads that evening.

Airport parking is usually a pain in the butt, but doable. However, because the van is a "high top" it is too tall to fit in the airport garage. We had decided that Roberta would go in and find the travelers while I sat in the van. I parked in the loading and unloading zone, ready to move it a few feet every ten minutes so I don't get ticketed. Many other people are apparently doing the same thing with normal sized vehicles. There is a constant flow of vehicles. A disproportionate number of said vehicles (pronounced "veehickles" by Floridians) are Lincoln Town Cars, piloted by old farts of both genders whose visual acuity and grasp of spatial relationships has headed somewhere south of adequate. Some of these pilots (and some of their crew members) are wearing the dark wrap-around glasses provided those recently subjected to corrective eye surgery. I get the impression of an assemblage of randomly moving, bipedal insects. Not surprisingly, these limitations coupled with the size of the veehickles results in a sort of jack-straw parking arrangement which leads to a breakdown of order and a mini-gridlock situation within ten minutes of my arrival.

I watched the situation evolve with bemused detachment until a uniformed, middle-aged woman with a pendulous bosom approached me. She said.

"Y'all gonna hafta move this veehickle."

"Yes, M' am. I'll be happy to, as soon as I can."

[looking at the tangle around me] "Yeah, ah see what you mean. These old fart Yankee snowbirds [me??] come down heuh, they buy the biggest veehickle they can find, and then they all come here pickin' up moah Yankees and makin' me crazy. Yes, suh. Makin' me crazy. [yelling two cars down] Hey, Mr. LTJ [license plate] don't you go bashin' into that veehickle! [to me] Lord, lord, Ah'm gonna hafta sort this out."

Good luck. There are three Town Cars, a Cadillac, a Dodge mini-van and a Subaru all in a knot of conflicting angles behind a bus. Some of them are driverless, while the passengers of others are outside them trying to direct the overtaxed driver to a path of freedom.

"Hey, Hey, Hey, Mr. AHP!! ... Wait for Mr. DX to clear before you pull out!!"

Mr. AHP is a Town Car operated by a white-haired, long-nosed insect, with a cigarette stuck in his face. He hits the brakes hard enough to cause the Town Car to halt in a tire-shrieking dive; pauses as Mr. DX clears; then hammers the throttle; burning rubber and giving big bosom the finger as he lunges away.

"Well, thank you very much too, Mr. AHP. ... What's that stand for? Asshole puke face? Well, ah nevuh. You believe that? ... Asshole!"

She's obviously annoyed, and as she moves off to take charge of the re- maining mess, I see that the arrivals have ... well... arrived. I greet them, help my mother into the van, and look around for the Patra. She has picked up a phone and is dialing (pushing buttons). "Who are you calling?" I ask.

"I have to call David." [She doesn't refer to him as "the Me."]

"Why?"

"Because, he insisted that I call as soon as we got here."

"Can't it wait 'til we get to the house? I have a phone."

"No, I have to call him now or I won't hear the end of it."

"What's the big deal?"

"Hey, I don't know. He's **your** brother! He made me promise I'd call as soon as we landed. [I give her a quizzical look] Hey, don't ask me! Do **you** want to talk to him?"

"No!"

With repeated assurances such as "fine, good, okay, yes, alright," she as- suages the Me's concerns. He's apprehensive, but she makes cooing noises at him, confirming that we (particularly my mother) are all in fine fettle. She asserts the obvious fact that there is nothing he can do about our situation in any event, and that we are all big people with sufficient cumulative experi- ence and intelligence to effectively manage the care and feeding of our mother. This done, we gather in our veehickle. I bid farewell to big bosom, receive a big, toothy, head-shaking grin in response, and head home. As we proceed, I advise Patra and Paul of the uncertainty of sleeping accommoda- tions. They don't care; they're happy to be here. As long as Ma has a bed, there's no problem. This is a good attitude. Things must be looking up. I know my speed and location.

Evan is at the house. He and Lou have assembled the waterbeds. The pedestals are not wood, but at this point I'm not going to demand that they be disassembled. One of the beds is full and the other is filling by means of a hose. Evan wants his check. I give him a check with a short commentary on my something less than complete satisfaction, which I tell him he can allevi- ate by leaving my house. He leaves. After the luggage was brought in and we were more or less settled, I decided to check the status of the bed.

Despite the fact that I had the proper device for the hose-to-bed connec- tion, and that he had used this device to fill the first bed, Evan had not seen fit to utilize the device on the second bed. Instead, he had simply placed the end of the hose into the opening. As the mattress filled, it became elevated and while (perhaps, because) no one was watching, the hose slipped from the filler tube. Several gallons of water had not entered the mattress. Those gallons were now elsewhere. With a measured amount of cursing I shut off the water, fetched the shop vac and spent the next half hour removing the misdirected water.

The next day, two guys showed up for the purposes of removing the parquet floor and replacing the rugs. Although it was December, it was warm and humid. Removal was to be by way of hammers and chisels, because the mastic used to bond the wood to the cement floor could not be broken otherwise. Thinking of comfort, I turned on the air conditioner. It made satisfying noises, but failed to cool. I apologized to the two guys and asked if they had heard of Heisenberg.

They hadn't, although one of the guys ventured that he might be a contractor working out of New Smyrna. The work began. It became clear that the rate at which progress was being made was insufficient to complete the task in a single day. I, therefore, joined in with my own hammer and (since I had no suitable chisel) screwdriver in an attempt to increase the manpower and provide encouragement to the two guys to pick up the pace.

Roberta and our guests headed out for an extended shopping/sightseeing tour.

The area to be cleared of flooring was approximately 16' by 10'. This is a rather small space to accommodate three guys swinging hammers. We worked as far from each other as possible to avoid mishaps, but there would be several near misses. With activity in full swing, my mother-in-law appeared. She's wearing pink polyester slacks, white socks with off-white walking shoes and a flowered, short-sleeved blouse stuck into the elastic waistband of the slacks. She's holding her pocketbook close to her side with one hand and dangling the ever present Players 100s cigarette in the other, standing in the middle of the work area like some potbellied, candy cane.

"What ah ya doin'?"

"Trying to work."

"Huh?"

"We have to get the wood up before the rug goes down."

"Oh. I wanted to see the rug."

"You can see it. It's in the truck."

"No. I mean, I want ta see it in."

"So do I. It's not."

[one of the guys] "Lady. Don't stand there, OK?"

[ignoring the guy] "Where's Berta?"

"She's not here."

"Wheyah did she go?"

"She took my relatives out. She wanted to stay out of our way so we could work."

"Why didn't she call me?"

"You should ask her that question."

[the other guy] "Hey, Lady, I don't mean to be rude, but if you don't move you could get hurt."

[ignoring the other guy] "Well, jeez, you guys ah shoowah makin' a mess. How long is it gonna take?"

"The whole time."

"Oh. ... When's Berta gettin' back?"

"When she gets here."

"Oh. ... Well, I went ta the doctuh's this mornin'. [sighing - talking to the other guy, who made the mistake of making eye contact] Yeah, I hafta have a foot taken outta my colon."

[the other guy] "Really? How did it get there?"

"Huh? ... Yeah. ... Well, I might. I don't know. It's got a kink in it."

[the guy] "The foot?"

"Yeah.... No! What has?"

[the other guy] "The foot has a kink?"

"I don't know, but it's got a kink in it. Jezzuz chrise, don't nobody unnerstan' English aroun' heyuh? It's in my colon!"

[the guy] "Lady, if you don't move you could have more than a foot in your colon."

"Oh, am I in the way? Well, I'm gonna go, I suppose. I wanted ta see the rug, but if it ain't down, well, I guess I'll see it latuh. So, tell Berta I was heyuh. Jezzuz, it's hot in heyuh. Why doncha turn on thuh ayuh?"

"Golly, that's a good idea. Why didn't one of you guys think of that?"

"See? Yowuh mothuh-in-law's good for somethin', Ronnie."

"Bye, Ma."

She left. The guy said,

"No offense, but what the hell was that?"

"My mother-in-law."

"Jesus Christ, I was getting ready to roll her up in the goddamn rug and throw her in the canal."

"I'd pay to see that."

The guys and I worked on ripping out the floor, making a lot of noise, making a mess and sweating profusely: man stuff. We finished clearing away the wood. The guys started putting down the rugs, but weren't finished when Roberta, et al. returned from the shopping spree. The guys finally finished and left after six o'clock.

With the house under control (more or less) we were free to do something more traditional; i.e., go to Disney. We had made arrangements to meet two women that we know ("the twins") at Epcot. The reason for this is the twins have worked for Disney for more than fifteen years and are, thus, eligible to have "guests" visit the park "free-for-nothing." This is a good thing because I am completely Disneyed out, and if I had to pay to get in I'd probably never visit the place again. I don't mean that I don't enjoy it; just that after you've done Disney a dozen times, there is little incentive to go back.

In any event, we met the twins at about 9 a.m. They handled the necessary process; even provided a wheelchair for my mother. She, as you might expect, objected to this means of locomotion, but we insisted, knowing what a trek the park can be. I have referred (I believe) previously to dragging children, grandchildren and their attendant paraphernalia around the park as the "Disney death march." This escapade would be different in that regard. With three other able-bodied adults, all five adults capable of reason and speech, and all in control of bowel and urinary functions, most causes of warranted and unwarranted concern, frustration, anxiety, whining, confusion and chaotic behavior would be absent or manageable.

The presence of the wheelchair had a distinctly salutary effect in three ways. First, the burden of walking was significantly reduced for my mother. Second, three others shared the burden of relocating her from ride to ride. Third, and perhaps most important, pushing a person in a wheelchair at Disney has a profound effect on Disney employees (or whatever they are). What I mean is that whenever we approached the entrance of an "attraction," a seemingly human entity would suddenly appear. From where, I don't know. They would just appear, sometimes from the side, sometimes in front of us, but always as if they had been beamed to the spot by some subterranean teleportation device. I don't know how they knew where we were or where we were headed or what our speed might be, but one would materialize and beckon us to follow. We followed, and through a previously unnoticed doorway and side chamber would emerge at the head of the line. Such preferential treatment is afforded to the chair bound person and his/her entire entourage.

We did all of the Magic Kingdom by 4 o ' clock. We did everything we wanted to do at Epcot by about 8 o'clock. America! What a country.

I won't bore you with any detail on the other touristy things to which we subjected the relatives. I will note that we couldn't take them for the usual nature and wildlife boat tour through the local canals. The reason being that my boat's motor, which had been operating perfectly until then, decided to cease operations - probably because I was observing it. Fortunately, the problem wasn't a matter of electrons, protons, quarks, gluons, mesons, nuclei, etc. It was a straightforward mechanical failure. "A simple matter of fatigue," the mechanic said, grinning with the confidence of a practicing Newtonian. Right. Like he knows anything.

I think that some quanta which had been acting like particles, decided to act like waves - just one man's opinion.

I can see by the page count that this has gone on quite long enough, so I'll stop for now. Before I close, however, I want you to know that while we were disappointed that you were unable to visit, we certainly understand. We all hope that Aunt Virginia is doing well and that you are taking care of yourself. I'll be calling you.